Separation and Retirement Incentives in the Federal Civil Service

A Comparison of the Federal Employees Retirement System and the Civil Service Retirement System

Beth J. Asch

John T. Warner

Prepared for the
Office of the Secretary of Defense

National Defense Research Institute

RAND

Responding to policy analysis needs of the Deputy Assistant Secretary of Defense for Civilian Personnel Policy (DASD(CPP)), RAND is currently conducting a series of studies on civilian personnel management issues. This study, which is part of that larger RAND effort, examines the Federal Employees Retirement System (FERS) and the Civil Service Retirement System (CSRS) to determine what incentives each includes for turnover and retirement. In addition, it compares actual separation outcomes under FERS with those under CSRS for early- and mid-career DoD civil service personnel. The study should be of interest to policymakers and researchers concerned with the personnel outcomes produced by these two large federal compensation systems.

This report was prepared under the sponsorship of the Office of Civilian Personnel Policy, Office of the Under Secretary of Defense for Personnel and Readiness. It was prepared within the Forces and Resources Policy Center of RAND's National Defense Research Institute, a federally funded research and development center sponsored by the Office of the Secretary of Defense, the Joint Staff, the unified commands, and the defense agencies.

CONTENTS

Appendix

TABLES

In 1987 a new retirement system for civil service personnel was introduced. Called the Federal Employees Retirement System (FERS), it consists of three parts: a defined benefit plan (the Basic Plan) that bases retirement benefits on the employee's earnings and years of service (YOS), Social Security coverage, and a defined contribution plan called the Thrift Savings Plan (TSP). Both employees and their employing agencies contribute to the TSP, and the value of the employee's retirement benefit depends on how the TSP performs over time.

Some observers (e.g., Congressional Budget Office, 1986; U.S. Office of Personnel Management (see Johnston, 1988); and General Accounting Office, 1990) have claimed that FERS would alter some of the separation and retirement patterns observed under FERS predecessor, the Civil Service Retirement System (CSRS). First, these observers hypothesized that CSRS produced insufficient turnover among those in their mid-careers. Insufficient turnover can be a problem if it prevents the hiring or promotion of better-trained or more-skilled personnel, or if it dulls the efforts and retention incentives of high-quality junior personnel by allowing mid- and late-career personnel to block promotion opportunities for others. By moving to FERS, these observers thought that more separations would be produced among those in their mid and late careers.

Second, CSRS was viewed as causing senior personnel, such as those in managerial positions, to retire as soon as they became eligible rather than inducing them to wait to retire at later ages. When senior personnel retire at the first age of retirement eligibility (age 55 under CSRS), two costs can be imposed on the civil service: the direct cost of finding a qualified replacement and the indirect cost of subordinates whose productivity may be reduced while a qualified replacement is being found. By moving to FERS, it was hypothesized that senior personnel would be induced to defer retirement beyond their first retirement-eligible age.

Little research has been conducted to prove whether FERS embeds separation and retirement incentives that are consistent with these hypotheses. The research presented in this report seeks to fill this gap. Specifically, the research addresses the following questions:

1. Which system is more generous in terms of increasing expected net lifetime wealth: FERS or CSRS?

2. What are the retirement age incentives embedded in each system? Do those covered by FERS have an incentive to retire at later ages than those covered by CSRS?

3. Are separation incentives for mid-career and senior personnel stronger under FERS than under CSRS? Do we observe higher separation rates among early and mid-careerists who are under FERS than among those under CSRS?

In the second half of 1998, those covered by CSRS were allowed to switch to FERS apparently because of the tremendous growth in stock market returns in recent years, and the beneficial effect of this growth on TSP returns. Switching would allow their federal retirement benefits to reflect future growth in stock market returns. Therefore, we also address this question:

4. Who is better off financially by switching to FERS: New hires, mid-careerists, or senior personnel?

To address these questions, we first simulate and compare the expected net lifetime wealth under FERS and under CSRS at each leaving age for a "representative" individual. We then infer from these simulation results the separation, retirement, and switch incentives embedded in CSRS and in FERS. To conduct the simulations, we make assumptions about various underlying factors, such as the inflation rate, the average rate of return on TSP accumulations, the individual's personal discount rate, the individual's TSP contribution rates over his or her career, the individual's pay profile, and his or her minimum retirement age under FERS. To examine how our results would vary under alternative assumptions, we also perform a sensitivity analysis. We then analyze time-series cross-sectional data from the Defense Manpower Data Center on DoD civil service personnel from fiscal year (FY) 82 through FY96 to examine the effect of FERS on empirical separation rates for junior and mid-career personnel. We focus our empirical analysis on junior and mid-career civil service personnel because insufficient time has passed since FERS was introduced to examine the separation and retirement rates of senior personnel who have spent their entire careers under FERS rather than under CSRS. We also exclude from our empirical analysis those who voluntarily switched to FERS during the 1980s because their decision to switch may have been based on characteristics, unrelated to the separation incentives embedded in FERS, that made them more or less likely to separate from the civil service.

GENEROSITY

We find that expected net lifetime wealth is higher under FERS than under CSRS under a variety of alternative assumptions. In addition, we find that the relative advantage of FERS is even greater for those who enter the civil service at later ages, because the Social Security system includes a windfall elimination provision that partially deducts the employee's Social Security benefit for his or her CSRS annuity. The deduction is larger for those who enter the civil service at older ages because they usually have some Social Security–covered employment. Therefore, for these individuals, FERS is more attractive than CSRS.

The fact that we find FERS to be more generous is *not* a result of the enormous growth in stock market returns in recent years and the implied beneficial effect on TSP returns. Our base analysis assumes a conservative 6 percent real growth rate in TSP returns, a rate that is far below the real overall performance of the stock market in recent years. Rather, net expected wealth is greater under FERS because of a combination of factors—including the accumulation of benefits from three retirement systems; the opportunity to earn an average rate of return on the TSP, which can protect the fund accumulation from the erosive effects of inflation over time; Social Security coverage; and the lack of a windfall elimination provision for those covered by FERS.

RETIREMENT INCENTIVES

We also find that FERS and CSRS embed identical retirement age and YOS incentives, given our assumption of a minimum retirement age under FERS of 55. Given this assumption, our simulations show that expected net lifetime wealth is maximized at the same age and YOS under both retirement systems. Therefore, from a financial standpoint, individuals who enter civil service and are covered by FERS would choose to retire at the same age and YOS as similar individuals who enter civil service and are covered by CSRS, given our assumptions. This similarity in retirement incentives is notable because it is contrary to one of the initial intents of FERS, which was to embed incentives to retire later. However, the minimum retirement age under FERS rises with birth year and is age 57 for those born after 1970. When the minimum is 57, we find that individuals who spend their careers in the civil service will retire later (at age 57 versus age 55) if they are covered by FERS than if they are covered by CSRS. Since recent hires are more likely to be born after 1970 than earlier hires, our analysis predicts that recent hires will tend to retire at a later age under FERS than they would have retired had they been covered under CSRS. Therefore, FERS will successfully tend to induce more recent hires to delay retirement beyond age 55.

Because of nonmonetary factors, such as ill health or a particularly good job assignment in the civil service, individuals may choose to retire either before or after the age and YOS at which their expected net lifetime wealth is maximized. However, those who do leave before or after the wealth-maximizing age will suffer a financial penalty. We find that the size of this penalty is smaller under FERS. Those who retire earlier or who retire later than the optimal age will not lose as much in net wealth under FERS by failing to retire at the wealth-maximizing retirement age. The penalty is lower under FERS for those who leave *before* the wealth-maximizing retirement point because FERS offers more inflation protection for those who leave before they are eligible for normal retirement, and FERS allows such individuals to receive deferred retirement pay at an earlier age. The penalty is lower under FERS for those who leave *after* the wealth-maximizing point because the total retirement benefit under FERS increases more with YOS and earnings than does the benefit under CSRS.

Since the penalty is lower, our analysis suggests that FERS will create more variance in retirement ages, although the average retirement age is predicted to be the same under FERS given an assumed minimum retirement age of 55. In other words, under FERS more individuals will retire earlier and more will retire later than the wealth-maximizing retirement age. Therefore, while FERS is more likely to encourage senior personnel to stay in the civil service rather than retire at age 55, or more generally at the minimum retirement age, it is also more likely to encourage them to leave earlier. This aspect of FERS is not consistent with earlier hypotheses about the retirement incentives embedded in FERS. If the goal is to retain more senior personnel, then the retirement system needs to be constructed in such a way that the optimal retirement age shifts up for them.

SEPARATION INCENTIVES

Our simulation analysis finds that individuals covered by FERS have a stronger incentive to stay in the civil service than those covered by CSRS if they are at the beginning or middle of their careers but a weaker incentive to stay if they are nearing retirement. This result suggests that the separation incentives embedded in FERS are consistent only with prevailing hypotheses for those nearing retirement and not for those personnel in their early and mid-careers.

The reason why incentives to stay are stronger (separation incentives are weaker) under FERS for early- and mid-career personnel is that FERS is a more generous system. As an analytic exercise, we redefined FERS to exclude the Basic Plan and include only Social Security and the TSP as a means of making FERS a less generous system. In contrast to our original results, when FERS is redefined to be less generous, we find that junior and mid-career personnel have a weaker incentive to stay in the civil service. Therefore, had FERS been made less generous when it was introduced, the separation incentives embedded in it would have been consistent with earlier suggestions about the separation incentives in FERS.

SWITCH INCENTIVES

In our simulation of the decision to switch from CSRS to FERS, we find that individuals who face the switch decision early in their careers increase their expected net lifetime wealth at retirement if they switch to FERS. Those who face the switch decision late in their careers do not. They are better off by remaining under CSRS because those who start FERS later in their careers have fewer years in which to increase their TSP accumulations. In addition, CSRS retirement benefits grow with YOS in a nonlinear fashion because the multiplier in the benefits formula rises with YOS. As a result, individuals with more YOS under CSRS have more to lose by switching to FERS.

However, if those individuals facing a switch decision later in their careers do not anticipate staying in the civil service until retirement, then they may be better off financially if they switch to FERS. Therefore, whether or not those facing a switch decision in their mid- or late careers should switch to FERS depends on their career expectations, all else equal.

EMPIRICAL RESULTS

To examine how FERS affects separation outcomes of junior and mid-career personnel, we compare the annual separation rates in the late 1980s and 1990s of those covered by FERS with the annual separation rates in the early 1980s of those covered by CSRS. Since differences in separation rates of those covered by FERS compared with those covered by CSRS might be attributed to a "time effect"—i.e., changes that have occurred in the general environment between the early 1980s and the late 1980s and early 1990s—and not to differences in retirement system coverage, we create a control group to capture the "time effect." We proxy the control group with a group of senior civil service personnel who were covered by CSRS in both the early and later periods. We assume that any difference in the separation rates of this group between the early 1980s and the late 1980s and early 1990s captures the "time effect."

We estimate that separation rates under FERS for junior and mid-career civil service personnel are substantially lower then they are for similar personnel under CSRS. Given an estimated separation rate of 4.4 percent for those covered by CSRS, we estimate that FERS would reduce this rate to 2.4 percent, a difference of 45 percent. While this figure might overestimate the difference in the separation rates of those covered by FERS compared with those covered by CSRS because of some methodological issues that could not be addressed, it indicates that FERS is not producing *greater* separation rates among junior and mid-career personnel, as initially was thought would happen, and is likely to be producing substantially lower rates.

CONCLUSIONS

When FERS was introduced, some civil service workers expressed concern that FERS would provide smaller benefits than would CSRS for employees who planned to remain in the civil service until retirement. Our results suggest that these worries were generally groundless. Expected lifetime earnings and retirement wealth is predicted to be greater under FERS under a variety of alternative assumptions. These greater benefits might compensate civil service personnel for the risk they bear because their fund accumulations or the return on the accumulation might fall as a result of a downturn in the stock market or interest rates.

Nonetheless, the generosity of FERS gives junior and mid-career employees an incentive to stay that is stronger than it would have been had they been covered by CSRS. Empirically, we find evidence consistent with this simulation result. That is, we find that separation rates of junior and mid-career civil service personnel covered by FERS are as much as 45 percent lower than the rates for personnel covered by CSRS. These results suggest that turnover targets for junior and mid-career personnel need to be pursued outside of the retirement benefits package since the current retirement systems are not producing the desired turnover results. Determining how effective other forms of compensation, such as separation pay, would be in meeting these targets is an area for future research.

Another implication of our analysis is that FERS will be more successful than CSRS at inducing individuals to retire later in future years. Although FERS and CSRS embed the same retirement incentives for most current employees, recent hires will face a higher minimum retirement age under FERS (age 57). Consequently, our analysis predicts that recent (young) hires will retire at a later age under FERS than they would have retired under CSRS.

Our analysis also has implications for the switch window that was open during the later half of 1998 for employees covered by CSRS. Estimates indicate that about 4 percent of CSRS employees switched in 1987 when switching was also allowed. How many switched in 1998 depended critically on worker expectations about future real rates of returns on the TSP.[1] Given our assumption of a 6 percent real return on the TSP, our simulation analysis indicates that only those covered by CSRS who face the switch decision early in their careers would be unilaterally better off financially by switching to FERS. However, this was not the case for those covered by CSRS in 1998. They were not in their early careers but had at least 14 YOS. Our analysis suggests that whether individuals such as these are better off by switching to FERS depends on whether they plan to stay until they retire. If they do, our analysis indicates that they would be financially worse off by switching to FERS, given our assumption of a 6 percent real return of the TSP fund.

However, this result is sensitive to our assumption about TSP growth rates. At higher assumed rates, such as a 15 percent real return, we predict that those in their mid- and late careers *would* be better off financially by switching. Therefore, whether a large or trivial number of individuals switched to FERS in 1998 should depend crucially on what these individuals believed about the future real return on their TSP accumulation. Given the enormous growth in stock market returns in recent years, individuals facing the switch decision may have believed that such returns could be earned over the rest of their careers. In that case, larger numbers than might otherwise be expected may have choosen to switch to FERS. Since FERS costs more than CSRS to the employing agencies, differences in the number of personnel who switched could have important cost implications for these civil service agencies.

---

[1] There were no data yet available for 1998 as of the writing of this report.

We gratefully acknowledge the assistance of the Defense Manpower Data Center and specifically the help of Mike Dove, Jim Creager, and Deborah Eitelberg. At RAND, we would like to thank our programmer Rachel Louie for her assistance and our project leader Al Robbert for his valuable comments. We are also grateful to Jacob Klerman for providing the ideas behind our estimation approach and to Stan Panis and Craig College for their useful reviews. We benefited greatly from the comments and input of Dr. Larry Lacy, our project monitor and from the comments of the reviewers from the Civilian Personnel Management System Policy Support and Field Advisory Services (B&E). Finally, we appreciate the input and support of our project sponsor, Dr. Diane Disney, Deputy Assistant Secretary of Defense for Civilian Personnel Policy.

Chapter One

INTRODUCTION

In 1987, the federal government adopted a new retirement system for civil service workers. All employees hired since 1984 were placed under the new system, called the Federal Employees Retirement System (FERS), while existing employees remained under the old system, called the Civil Service Retirement System (CSRS).

CSRS is a defined benefit retirement plan in which the employee's retirement benefits depend on earnings and years of service (YOS). Because CSRS was begun in the 1920s before the advent of Social Security, employees covered by CSRS were not covered by the Social Security system.[1] FERS differs from CSRS in fundamental ways. It includes not only a less generous defined benefit plan called the "Basic Plan," but also Social Security coverage and a defined contribution plan called the Thrift Savings Plan (TSP). Under the TSP, employees make contributions to the plan that are matched to some extent by the government.[2] These contributions are invested, and the value of the employee's retirement benefit under the TSP depends on how the investment fund performs over time.[3]

The adoption of FERS was in part motivated by the fundamental changes that were made to the Social Security system in the early 1980s. An important goal of policymakers in designing FERS was to include federal civil service workers in the Social Security system. First, policymakers wanted to address the perceived inequity caused by the lack of Social Security coverage for these workers. Second, they wanted to address a "double dipping" problem. Highly paid individuals could leave the civil service and work in the Social Security–covered sector sufficiently long to accumulate the minimum 40 quarters needed to qualify for Social Security benefits. Because of the progressive nature of the Social Security benefit formula, these work-

---

[1]A detailed description of CSRS and FERS is given in Appendix A.

[2]See Appendix A for the matching rates.

[3]Between 1987 and 1988, the federal government allowed those covered by CSRS and who left the civil service but were rehired after 1984 and had more than 5 years of service as of December 31, 1986, or as of the last break in covered service and at least one day of CSRS coverage the opportunity to switch to FERS within 6 months of their rehire date (as long as the new appointment is not excluded by law or regulation). If excluded, the employee would be covered by Federal Insurance Contributions Act (FICA) only. Those who opt not to switch to FERS when they return are covered by a system called CSRS-Offset. CSRS-Offset consists of two parts: CSRS and Social Security. Because of the enormous growth in the returns to TSP funds invested in the stock market since the early 1990s, pressure mounted on Congress in 1997 to open a conversion window yet again to give CSRS employees another opportunity to switch to FERS. Consequently, a six-month conversion window was open to existing CSRS-covered personnel in 1998.

ers could get higher benefits than they would have received had they worked their entire careers in covered Social Security employment. This problem was addressed by including Social Security in FERS and by creating the windfall elimination provision for those covered by CSRS. Under this provision, the employee's Social Security benefits are reduced by up to 40 percent of his or her CSRS benefits.

FERS was also adopted to address the substantial unfunded liability that CSRS generated (General Accounting Office (GAO), 1998). CSRS is funded from contributions of 14 percent of payroll—7 percent each from the employee and from the employing agency, but these payments are inadequate to cover the current (and future) liability of the system.[4] Estimates of the unfunded liability vary, but they indicate that for the system to be self-financing, the percentage of an employee's salary that must be put aside for each year of service (i.e., the "normal cost") would have to be over 25 percent, rather than the current 14 percent (GAO, 1998; Leonard, 1985). Under FERS, the current CSRS unfunded liability would still exist, but no additional unfunded liability would be created by the hiring of new employees because the TSP does not generate an unfunded liability.[5]

In addition to the problems of Social Security coverage and cost, several observers have suggested that CSRS also might produce undesirable retention and retirement behavior (Congressional Budget Office, 1986; Johnston, 1988; General Accounting Office, 1990; Mace and Yoder, 1995; Office of the Secretary of Defense (OSD), 1997). Some of these observers hypothesized that FERS would address these problems by changing the separation and retirement incentives of civil service personnel.

More specifically, CSRS has been thought to create "golden handcuffs," meaning that it imposes a substantial cost to those leaving in their mid- or late careers. CSRS allows deferred retirements only at age 62. In addition, CSRS benefits are based on the employee's highest three years' average salary and are not protected from any erosion of benefits from inflation that may occur between the dates of separation and retirement.[6] Consequently, those who leave prior to becoming retirement eligible substantially reduce the discounted present value (DPV) of their future retirement benefits. This penalty for leaving before a retirement-eligible age seemed to explain what was viewed as excessively low turnover among mid- and late-career personnel covered by CSRS.

From a personnel management standpoint, insufficient turnover among mid-career and senior personnel can prevent the hiring of younger personnel into the civil service and the associated rejuvenation of the workforce (Asch and Warner, 1994). Golden handcuffs are also a problem when those who stay excessively long block the

---

[4]The contribution rate will rise in 1999–2002, as discussed in Appendix A.

[5]In establishing FERS, Congress made a deliberate trade-off: increased charges to annual FERS expenditures for adding to the long-term CSRS retirement fund liability. In doing so, Congress has placed a new risk on the employees covered by FERS—their fund accumulations or the return on the accumulations might fall.

[6]While not always true, the employee's highest three years' salary is usually the final three years' salary. Also, since CSRS offers those with more than one year of service and fewer than five YOS the option to cash out their contributions with interest if they leave, CSRS offers some inflation protection to these individuals.

promotion opportunities and therefore the efforts and retention incentives for more-junior personnel. It is also a problem in high-skill jobs if those who are locked into civil service employment do not possess adequate skills or supply sufficient effort.

It is possible that FERS increases turnover and separation rates among mid-careerists and those nearing retirement age. Since those who separate under FERS could continue to earn an average return from the TSP, which tends to protect the fund from the erosive effects of inflation, and could continue to accumulate Social Security benefits in other covered employment, and since FERS allows for deferred retirements at younger ages, FERS may address the golden-handcuff problem associated with CSRS.

At the same time that CSRS seemed to create golden handcuffs for mid- and late-career personnel, it seemed to some observers to induce excessive retirement at the first normal retirement-eligible age. For example, individuals covered by CSRS with 30 YOS tend to retire at age 55 when they are first eligible, rather than wait to retire at later ages. The exodus of personnel at the first retirement-eligible point is problematic when there are some occupational areas or groups of workers whom the civil service would prefer to retire later, ex post. For example, finding qualified replacements for senior personnel in managerial positions who retire at age 55 can be costly and difficult. By introducing FERS, it was thought that the reward to highly skilled senior leaders of postponing their retirement beyond their first retirement-eligible age would be increased (or the penalty reduced).

Despite the suggestion that FERS produces greater separation incentives among mid-career and senior personnel and more deferred retirements among retirement-eligible personnel, little is actually known about the separation and retirement incentives embedded in FERS compared with those in CSRS. Also, little is known empirically about how separation outcomes differ under FERS compared with those under CSRS for similar groups of workers. The research presented in this report attempts to fill this gap. We assess the separation and retirement incentives embedded in FERS compared with those in CSRS to determine whether they are consistent with prevailing hypotheses about the separation and retirement incentives embedded in FERS. In addition, given that CSRS employees had an open enrollment season between July 1, 1998, and December 31, 1998, when they could have switched to FERS, it is of interest also to address the question of which personnel had an incentive to switch. Civil service employees also had the option to switch to FERS after FERS became operational in 1987. More specifically, we address the following questions:

1. Which system is more generous in terms of increasing expected net lifetime wealth: FERS or CSRS?

2. What are the retirement age incentives embedded in each system? Do those covered by FERS have an incentive to retire at later ages than those covered by CSRS?

3. Are separation incentives for mid-career and senior personnel stronger under FERS than under CSRS? Do we observe higher separation rates among early and mid-careerists who are under FERS than for those under CSRS?

4. Who is better off financially by switching to FERS: New hires, mid-careerists, or senior personnel?

To address these questions, we do simulations of the expected net lifetime earnings and retirement wealth that an employee would accumulate at each leaving age under FERS compared with each under CSRS. We then use this information to make inferences about the retirement and separation incentives embedded in each system. We use a simulation approach because we cannot learn much about lifetime retirement and separation incentives under FERS compared with those under CSRS by looking at actual data on those under each system. Since FERS has been in existence only since 1987 and covers those who entered since 1984, insufficient time has passed for an individual to have actually spent an entire work life and retired under FERS.

In addition to the simulation analysis, we also analyze time-series cross-sectional data on Department of Defense (DoD) civil service personnel. Since FERS has not been around long enough for someone to have spent a whole career in the civil service and retire under FERS, we limit the scope of the empirical analysis to examining differences in separation rates among those in their early and mid-careers.

The report is organized as follows. Chapter Two discusses how we simulate the expected net lifetime wealth under FERS compared with that under CSRS and how we infer separation and retirement incentives. Chapter Three presents the simulation results. In Chapter Four, we discuss the data we use, some confounding factors in our data analysis, and our empirical approach. Chapter Five presents our empirical findings. We summarize our findings and discuss policy implications in Chapter Six. The appendixes provide a summary of FERS and CSRS; a discussion about inconsistencies in DoD civilian personnel files regarding YOS; and variable definitions, descriptive statistics, and regression results.

Chapter Two

SIMULATION APPROACH AND ASSUMPTIONS

In this chapter, we describe our simulation approach and the assumptions we make to implement it. We use this approach to address questions about the relative generosity of FERS compared with that of CSRS, about the retirement and separation incentives embedded in each system, and the incentives to switch to FERS by those covered by CSRS.

The typical approach for comparing the relative generosity of benefits under different retirement systems is to compare their replacement rates at different retirement ages—the fraction of final pay that is covered by the retirement plan's annuity (see, for example, GAO, 1997). A problem with this approach is that the replacement rate does not easily account for differences in contribution rates between retirement systems. For example, the annuity under one system may be more generous, but if employees contribute more of their earnings to the system, their expected lifetime wealth may not be greater.

Replacement rates also do not account for differences in cost-of-living-adjustment (COLA) provisions between systems. For example, an annuity may be larger under one system and yield a higher replacement rate, but if it is not inflation protected, the overall value of the benefit could be lower. The replacement rate approach also does not account for what the individual could earn in alternative employment. A retirement system may be more generous in terms of its replacement rate, but so may the replacement rate in alternative employment, so the individual may not be better off. Other problems with the replacement rate approach are that it does not account for mortality risk or for the fact that the replacement rate may be higher at older retirement ages but the payout period shorter, resulting in potentially lower lifetime benefits.

Because of these flaws, we do not use replacement rates to compare benefits under FERS with those under CSRS. Instead we use a measure that accounts for such factors as mortality risk, contribution rates, payout length, COLA provisions, and the value of the alternative. Before developing our approach, we note that labor economists have developed several alternative models for analyzing retirement and separation decisions and for comparing the incentives embedded in alternative retirement systems. One class of models is based on stochastic dynamic programming (Gotz and McCall, 1980; Rust, 1989; and Daula and Moffitt, 1995). In stochastic dynamic programming models, the incentive to remain with an employer rather than separating or retiring may be shown to be a weighted average of the incentive to re-main one more period and then leave, two more periods and then leave, and so forth. Weights are based on the individual's probability of remaining to each future point and then separating. These probabilities depend, in turn, upon the individual's pref-erences and upon random shocks to the stay-leave decision at each point in time. Asch and Warner (1994) employ a version of the Gotz-McCall stochastic dynamic programming model to analyze the military compensation and personnel systems.

A simpler model is based upon deriving a future time horizon that is the focal point of current-period decisionmaking. This model has come to be known as the Annual-ized Cost of Leaving (ACOL) and is developed in detail in Warner and Goldberg (1984) and Black, Moffitt, and Warner (1990a and 1990b). Black, Moffitt, and Warner applied the model to the separation decisions of an entry cohort of DoD employees tracked for their first 10 years of employment. Lazear and Moore (1983) and Stock and Wise (1990) developed similar models of retirement decisions of workers in large firms.

ACOL is defined as the expected DPV of a person's lifetime earnings, net of his or her wealth accumulation in an alternative job, annuitized over the length of the em-ployment period. ACOL includes differences in future retirement pay and Social Se-curity accumulations. The rest of the report will often refer to ACOL as the expected net lifetime earnings and retirement wealth of the individual. Since ACOL is annu-itized DPV, it becomes the average annual pay differential between employment in the current job and the alternative.

In the economics literature, ACOL is also called the option value of staying in a given job. There has been much discussion about the relative strengths of the ACOL or option value approach and the stochastic dynamic programming approach (see the discussion in Stock and Wise, 1990; Lumsdaine, Stock, and Wise, 1992; and the ex-change between Gotz, 1990, and Black, Moffitt, and Warner, 1990a and 1990b). Be-cause we seek to describe only the retirement and separation incentives embedded in the two systems and do not attempt to estimate a structural model from actual data, we eschew the stochastic dynamic programming approach in favor of the sim-pler ACOL approach. This approach is well-suited for our purposes.

In both classes of models, nonmonetary factors also influence retirement and sepa-ration decisions. Models typically recognize two sources of nonmonetary distur-bances. One source is "permanent preference factors." Some jobs offer better working conditions and better amenities than do other jobs. Below, we let the sym-bol τ represent the value an individual places upon the nonpecuniary aspects of federal versus nonfederal employment. The other source arises from unexpected, or purely random, "shocks" to the retirement or separation decision. Poor health or an unexpectedly good job offer elsewhere are random factors that can cause even a per-son with strong preferences for the current employer (i.e., a high τ) to retire or sepa-rate.

In the remainder of this chapter, we describe more formally how the ACOL variable is defined, and we discuss how we infer retirement and separation incentives from the ACOL variables we compute. We then discuss the assumptions we make to computer simulate the ACOL values for a "representative" individual. These computer simulations allow us to analyze the retirement and separation incentives embedded in FERS compared with those in CSRS.[1]

DEFINING THE ACOL VARIABLE

To compute the ACOL, we subtract from the DPV of the employee's future earnings from staying the DPV of his or her future earnings (i.e., earnings wealth) if he or she leaves the civil service immediately. The net earnings and retirement wealth if the employee leaves includes the DPV of pay in the alternative sector, the DPV of the civil service retirement benefit he or she would be eligible for upon leaving immediately as of the current period, and the DPV of the Social Security benefits that the employee would be eligible for at retirement.[2] To account for differences in the length of time over which discounting is done when the career horizon changes, the net wealth measure is annuitized to create the ACOL variable. All dollars are discounted to the entry age.

Formally, we denote the cost of leaving today, at time t, compared with that of staying until a future time period N as COL(N,t). If S_N is the value of staying until period N, and L_t is the value of leaving today at time t, then COL(N,t) equals

$$COL(N,t) = S_N - L_t.$$

The value of leaving today, L_t, is given by

$$L_t = W_{tA} + R_{tC} + SS_t, \tag{2.1}$$

where

W_{tA} = DPV of alternative pay (net of Social Security contributions) from t until the person exits the labor force.

R_{tC} = DPV of civil service retirement benefits for which he or she would be eligible upon leaving at t.

SS_t = DPV of any Social Security benefits for which he or she would be eligible upon leaving at t.

The value of staying until a future period N is given by

---

[1]Our simulations focus on the provisions for immediate and deferred retirement under FERS and CSRS. They ignore the provisions for "early" retirement. The early retirement benefit is available in certain involuntary separation cases and in cases of voluntary separations during a reduction-in-force. Since our focus is on normal *voluntary* separation incentives, we ignore this part of FERS and CSRS.

[2]It should be noted that in computing the discounted present value of future retirement annuities we account for mortality risk in our calculations using a life table that gives the probability that an individual will survive to each age.

$$S_N = W_{N^C} + W_{N^A} + R_{N^C} + SS_N, \qquad (2.2)$$

where

W_{N^C} = DPV of civil service net pay (net of Social Security and retirement contributions) from t until period N.

W_{N^A} = DPV of alternative pay from N until the person exits the labor force at period T.

R_{N^C} = DPV of civil service retirement benefits for which he or she would be eligible upon leaving at N.

SS_N = DPV of Social Security benefits for which he or she would be eligible upon leaving at N.

Given these definitions, the COL(N,t) can be written as follows:

$$COL(N,t) = S_N - L_t = (W_{N^C} + W_{N^A} - W_{t^A}) + (R_{N^C} - R_{t^C}) + (SS_N - SS_t). \qquad (2.3)$$

The first right-side term in Eq. (2.3) is the difference between the DPV of earnings from a career path that includes staying N more years in the federal sector and then working T – N more years before withdrawal from the labor force ($W_N^C + W_N^A$) and the DPV of a T – t year career within alternative employment (W_t^A). The second term in Eq. (2.3) measures the increase in the DPV of retirement pay if the individual stays N – t more years rather than leaving immediately. Similarly, the third term measures the net change in the DPV of Social Security benefits as a result of N – t more years of employment in the federal sector.

Let $\beta = 1/(1 + \rho)$ where ρ is the individual's personal discount rate. Then, the annualized cost of leaving now rather than remaining N – t more periods is

$$ACOL(N,t) = \frac{COL(N,t)}{\sum\limits_{j=t+1}^{N} \beta^{j-t}}. \qquad (2.4)$$

Since ACOL(N,t) is the annuity equivalent of COL(N,t), ACOL(N,t) measures the average annual earnings differential between employment in the federal and nonfederal sectors, including not just pay differences while employed but also differences in expected future retirement benefits between sectors as well as differences due to Social Security accumulations.

DECISION RULE FOR DETERMINING OPTIMAL RETIREMENT AGE

Notice that there are T – t values of ACOL for a given individual: ACOL(t + 1,t), ACOL(t + 2,t), . . . , ACOL(T,t) or N – t values from ACOL(t + 1,t) through ACOL(N,t). To determine the optimal retirement age, we assume that the individual stands at the entry age (i.e., t is assumed to equal 1) and looks at every possible future career horizon N, calculates ACOL(N,1), and chooses the N or age where his or her expected ACOL(N,1) is maximized (denoted ACOL*(N,1)). At this point, the person will maximize his or her expected net earnings and retirement wealth over his or her lifetime relative to the entry age.

As will be discussed in the context of separation incentives, individuals may leave before the optimum career length once nonmonetary and random factors are considered. For example, if the individual receives an unexpectedly good outside opportunity that exceeds this maximum or if he or she finds that the disamenities of the civil service outweigh this maximum, then he or she will leave prior to the age when the ACOL is maximized. That is, the ACOL indicates the financial net gain to staying (or the financial cost of leaving) over the time horizon that maximizes wealth, but other factors can also influence the decision to leave.

As an example, Figure 2.1 graphs ACOL(N,1) for alternative N and shows the N at which we find ACOL*(N,1). For someone who enters at age 40, the maximized ACOL(N,1) is ACOL*(20,1), i.e., the ACOL is maximized at 20 YOS and age 60.

To compare retirement age incentives under FERS with those under CSRS, we simulate ACOL(N,1) for a representative individual under FERS and under CSRS, holding entry age constant. We then find the N where ACOL*(N,1) occurs for each system. If the maximized ACOL(N,1) occurs at the same N, we conclude that FERS and CSRS embed the same retirement age incentives, given our assumptions.

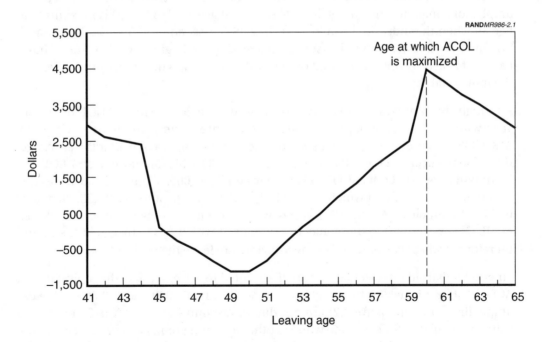

Figure 2.1—Annualized Cost of Leaving by Leaving Age

DECISION RULE FOR WHETHER TO SEPARATE AT A GIVEN AGE

Although the time horizon over which ACOL is maximized, $ACOL^*(N,1)$, indicates the optimal retirement point, it does not, by itself, indicate whether a person will remain until that point or separate. As noted above, preferences and such random factors as sudden ill health or an unexpectedly strong or weak economy will also affect the separation decision in period t.

To examine separation incentives at each t, we no longer set t equal to 1 as we do in our examination of retirement incentives. Instead, we let t vary, and we find $ACOL^*(N,t)$ for every t, given entry age. We then compare $ACOL^*(N,t)$ to the value of nonmonetary and random factors. Formally, if τ is an individual's net preference for federal employment and ε_t denote random shocks to the current-period separation decision, an individual remains in federal employment at time t if $ACOL^*(N,t) + \tau + \varepsilon_t > 0$ or $ACOL^*(N,t) > -(\tau + \varepsilon_t)$. In other words, the individual stays in period t if the maximum expected future annualized pay differential (or expected net lifetime wealth) exceeds his or her net preference for *non*federal employment plus the (negative of the) value of new shocks to the decision.

As the individual progresses through his or her career, he or she is assumed to compare $ACOL^*(N,t)$ with $\tau + \varepsilon_t$ when deciding whether to separate at time t. As it turns out in our simulation analysis of FERS and CSRS, we find that the age or the N at which $ACOL(N,t)$ is maximized does not generally vary with t. In other words, $ACOL^*(N,t)$ maximizes at the same N, for all t, holding entry age constant. For example, for someone who enters the civil service at age 20, $ACOL(N,t)$ is maximized at age 55 when the individual would have 35 YOS (i.e., N equals 35 at the maximum). We find that, if it was optimal to stay until age 55 at the beginning of the individual's career, it is usually optimal for him or her to stay until 55 as the career progresses and the individual ages.

Although the N at which $ACOL^*(N,t)$ occurs does not vary with t, $ACOL^*(N,t)$ does vary with t. For example, for someone who enters the civil service at age 20, $ACOL^*(35,1)$ may equal \$4,000 for someone contemplating leaving after the entry age. If the leaving decision is contemplated at age 30, $ACOL^*(35,10)$ may equal \$7,000. If it is contemplated at age 40, $ACOL^*(35,20)$ may equal \$13,000. Figure 2.2 illustrates this example. The age or N at which $ACOL^*(35,1)$, $ACOL^*(35,10)$, and $ACOL^*(35,20)$ occurs is 55. Nonetheless, $ACOL^*(35,t)$ varies with t when t equals 1, 10, or 20. Since $ACOL^*(N,t)$ varies with t, there may be some t's at which $ACOL^*(N,t) < -(\tau + \varepsilon_t)$ and therefore at which it is optimal for the individual to leave the civil service.

Since all dollars in our calculations are discounted to the entry age, the differences in $ACOL^*(N,t)$ as t varies (or the differences in \$4,000 and \$7,000 and \$13,000 in the example illustrated in Figure 2.2) are not due to discounting nor to the fact that one value is calculated for someone who is at the beginning of his or her career and the others are calculated for someone who is older. Rather, the differences are due to variations in the value of civil service retirement benefits and Social Security benefits in the alternative sector for someone thinking of leaving at age 30 or age 40 compared with someone thinking of leaving at age 20.

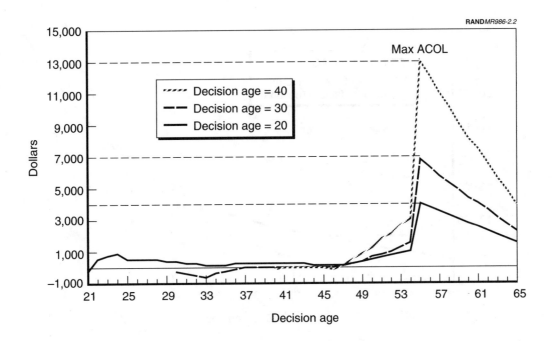

Figure 2.2—Example of ACOL at Different Separation Decision Ages, Entry Age = 20

In Figure 2.3 , we plot the ACOL*(N,t) for the different t's that are shown in Figure 2.2. For example, Figure 2.3 shows that for an individual at age 30, ACOL*(35,10) equals $7,000. The individual is assumed to choose to remain in federal service in period t if ACOL*(N,t) exceeds the value of nonmonetary factors, including preferences and random factors. For illustrative purposes, we assume that the value of nonmonetary factors is shaped like the gray curve in the example shown in Figure 2.3. In this example, the individual will stay until age 45 because ACOL*(N,t) exceeds the nonmonetary factors until that age. Beyond age 45, the value of nonmonetary and random factors exceeds the maximized net wealth that can be expected by the individual in the civil service.

To compare separation incentives under FERS with those under CSRS, we compare ACOL*(N,t) for all t, given entry age, under both systems. In other words, we simulate the values illustrated in Figure 2.3 for a representative individual under FERS compared with one under CSRS. If ACOL*(N,t) under FERS is greater than ACOL*(N,t) under CSRS for a given t, then the cost of leaving and the gain to staying is greater under FERS at that decision age. In this case, we would conclude that FERS embeds weaker separation incentives or stronger stay incentives at that decision age.

SIMULATION ASSUMPTIONS

To implement the ACOL approach discussed above, we need to make several assumptions that allow us to computer simulate the expected ACOL values under CSRS compared with those under FERS. These assumptions allow us to hypothesize a

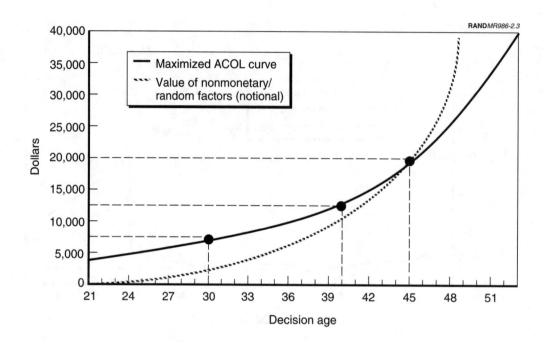

Figure 2.3—Example of Maximized ACOL and Value of Nonmonetary and Random Factors,
Entry Age = 20

"representative individual" working in the civil service under "representative" conditions. Specifically, we need to make assumptions about the individual's personal discount rate, the inflation rate over the individual's lifetime, the rate at which the individual's TSP fund will grow, the individual's entry salary level and growth rate over his or her career, the fraction of salary that the individual will contribute to the TSP over his or her career, and the minimum retirement age that the individual will face under FERS. The assumptions that we make are listed in Table 2.1. We call this set of assumptions the base case. At the end of Chapter Three, we discuss how our results vary when we vary these assumptions.

We assume an annual inflation rate of 3 percent. We also assume that the individual's personal discount rate is 5 percent. As discussed in Appendix A, the minimum retirement age (MRA) at which an individual can retire under FERS Basic Plan varies with birth year. We assume that the MRA is 55. We also assume that the Thrift Savings Plan grows at a real annual rate of 6 percent over the course of the individual's

Table 2.1

Assumptions Used in the Base Case

Inflation rate	3 percent
Real Thrift Savings Plan growth rate	6 percent
Personal discount rate	5 percent
Minimum retirement age (FERS)	Age 55
Employee contribution rates	Vary with age[a]

[a]See Thrift Savings Plan Board, 1997.

career. This assumed rate is far short of the actual real growth in the stock market portion of the TSP in recent years. Nonetheless, for someone forecasting what average growth in the TSP will be over his or her entire career, a 6 percent rate seems reasonable. We also assume that the individual's contribution rate to the TSP varies with age. We used average TSP contribution rates by age, which were obtained from the Thrift Savings Plan Board. Finally, we assume the real pay profile illustrated in Figure 2.4. The pay profile is based on the average grade of DoD civil service personnel by age and years of service. These averages were computed using data on DoD civil service personnel in 1996, obtained from the Defense Manpower Data Center (DMDC).[3] We applied these averages to the fiscal year (FY) 1997 civil service pay table to compute average earnings by age and YOS. In real FY97 dollars, the person starts out at $25,000 and ends at around $56,000.[4] Finally, we assume that the individual will exit the labor force at age 65. In other words, if an individual retires at, say, age 55, he or she is assumed to find a job for 10 years in the alternative sector.

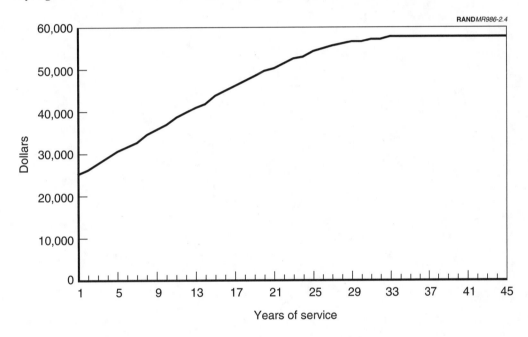

Figure 2.4—Assumed Real Pay Profile

---

[3]See Chapter Five for a more detailed data description.

[4]Ideally we should use the representative employee's expected earnings profile, which will most likely differ from the mean profile observed in the FY96 DMDC data because of selectivity biases. For example, if retirement and separation rates vary positively with earnings and YOS, then average earnings of those with more YOS in our cross-sectional data will be biased downward. As noted in the text, we conduct sensitivity analysis using alternative pay profiles to determine how our main results regarding the relative incentives embedded in FERS compared with those in CSRS are affected. As discussed in Chapter Three, our qualitative results are unchanged when a different pay profile is assumed. Therefore, we do not believe our main results are affected by using cross-sectional data to develop the assumed pay profile.

SIMULATION RESULTS

This chapter summarizes our simulation results. We first discuss which system is more generous in terms of providing greater ACOL values or expected net lifetime wealth, FERS or CSRS, at each leaving age. We then present our results regarding the retirement incentives and separation incentives embedded in each system. Next, we discuss the incentives to switch to FERS from CSRS. We conclude the chapter with a summary of the results of our sensitivity analysis. We conducted a sensitivity analysis to examine how our main simulation results would change if we varied the assumptions listed in Table 2.1 and Figure 2.4.

RELATIVE GENEROSITY

To determine under which retirement system the individual's expected net lifetime wealth is greater, we use our simulation approach to compare the expected ACOL values under FERS with those under CSRS at each possible leaving age.[1] Figure 3.1a shows the results for someone who enters at age 20, and Figure 3.1b shows the results for someone who enters at age 40. In both cases, the path of expected ACOL values under FERS lies above the path for CSRS for most leaving ages beyond the vesting point.[2] In other words, we find that net expected lifetime earnings and retirement wealth is greater for individuals covered by FERS. This result cannot be attributed to the enormous growth in stock market returns in recent years and the implied beneficial effect on TSP returns. As discussed in Chapter Two, we assume a conservative 6 percent real growth rate in TSP returns, a rate that is far below the real returns actually experienced in the stock market in recent years. Rather, net expected wealth is greater under FERS because of a combination of factors, including providing an average long-term rate of return on the TSP that tends to protect the fund accumulation from the erosive effects of inflation, Social Security coverage, and the lack of a Social Security windfall elimination provision for those covered by FERS.

---

[1]Personnel covered by CSRS are allowed to contribute to the TSP, but unlike those covered by FERS, their contributions are not matched by the employing agency. In a similar fashion, those covered by FERS can contribute to an Individual Retirement Account or Roth Individual Retirement Account, but their contributions are not matched by the employing agency. Our comparisons of FERS and CSRS do not include possible contributions to other retirement vehicles such as these or possible coverage by private-sector pension plans.

[2]The simulations account for the differing vesting points under the FERS basic plan and the TSP. (See Appendix A for a description of these components of FERS.)

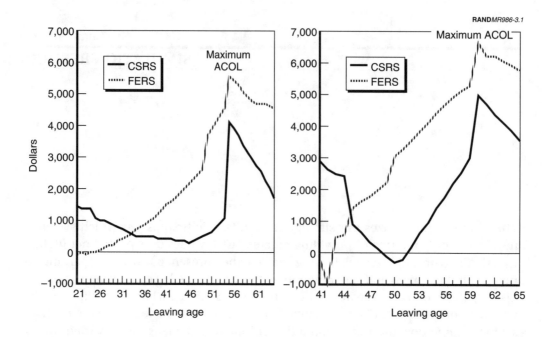

Figure 3.1a—Annualized Cost of Leaving Under Both Systems, Entry Age = 20

Figure 3.1b—Annualized Cost of Leaving Under Both Systems, Entry Age = 40

As discussed in Chapter Two, the decision rule for determining the expected optimal retirement age-YOS combination is to retire when the employee's expected ACOL is maximized. For someone entering at age 20, the simulation model predicts that the expected optimum is at age 55 with 35 YOS under both systems. For someone entering at age 40, the model predicts an optimum at age 60 with 20 YOS under both systems. As shown in each figure, we find that the maximum expected ACOL value is greater under FERS at the optimal retirement age-YOS combination. Therefore, those who retire under FERS at the optimal point will be better off financially on average, and this is especially true for late entrants—i.e., the gap between the maximum expected ACOL under FERS versus that under CSRS is greater for those who enter at age 40 than for those who enter at age 20.

The reason why FERS is even more generous for late entrants is that these individuals were employed in their earlier careers in covered employment and have a fairly sizable Social Security benefit accumulated. Given our assumption that individuals enter the labor market at age 20, those who enter the civil service at age 40 have 20 years of earlier covered employment. But because of the Social Security windfall elimination provision for those covered by CSRS, their accumulated Social Security retirement benefit is reduced significantly. The Social Security windfall elimination provision does not apply to those covered by FERS. Consequently, for someone who entered at a late age, expected net lifetime earnings and retirement wealth including Social Security is substantially lower under CSRS relative to that under FERS. Since those who enter civil service at age 20 do not have any accumulated Social Security benefits from their early careers, the Social Security windfall elimination provision for the early years does not affect their FERS-CSRS comparison.

That FERS is found to be more generous should alleviate concerns expressed by some that benefits under FERS would be smaller than those under CSRS. In addition, the greater benefits might compensate civil service personnel for the risk that their fund accumulations, or the returns on the accumulation, might fall when interest rates or the stock market falls.

RETIREMENT AGE-YOS INCENTIVES

To determine at which age-YOS combinations under FERS and CSRS individuals have an incentive to retire, the simulation model first computes the expected ACOL at each possible leaving age relative to leaving after the entry age. It then finds the age and YOS at which the expected ACOL is maximized. We conduct these simulations for different entry ages to determine whether FERS and CSRS embed different incentives for individuals with different career lengths. The simulation results are given in Table 3.1, which shows the expected optimal age and YOS of retirement under FERS and CSRS for different ages of entry into the civil service.

Holding entry age constant, we find that FERS and CSRS have identical retirement age-YOS incentives embedded in them regardless of career length, given our assumption of a minimum retirement age of 55 under FERS. For example, for those who enter the civil service at age 20, the incentive to retire is at age 55 with 35 YOS under both CSRS and FERS. For someone who entered at age 35, the incentive is to retire at age 60 with 25 years of service under both systems. This similarity in retirement age-YOS incentives is notable because, contrary to one of the initial intents of FERS, FERS and CSRS do not embed different optimal retirement incentives. However, as will be discussed in the context of our sensitivity analysis, when we assume a minimum retirement age of 57, the MRA for those who were born after 1970, we find that optimal retirement age for those who enter the civil service at age 20 under FERS is 57 rather than 55. In other words, retirement ages under FERS will automatically evolve to be older because of the rise in the MRA. Therefore, among recent entrants, FERS will successfully delay retirement to older ages relative to CSRS for those who enter the civil service at age 20 or 25.

One hypothesis regarding FERS was that it induces senior personnel such as managers to postpone retirement until later ages. The pay profile and TSP contribution rate assumptions underlying the results in Table 3.1 are for a median worker. Presumably, managers earn more than the median worker and contribute to the TSP at higher rates. To investigate whether we continued to find identical retirement age-YOS incentives embedded in FERS and CSRS for senior personnel, we reran our simulations assuming a significantly higher and steeper real pay profile and higher contribution rates. Specifically, we assume the individual begins employment at age 25 at $40,000 and that his or her pay grows to $95,000 in real dollars by the end of the career. The contribution rates we assume continue to vary by age but are about 40 percent higher than the ones we assume in the base case. For example, for individuals age 40 or older, we assume they contribute 6.4 percent of their earnings to the TSP instead of 4.5 percent, as in the base case. When we redo the analysis with these new assumptions, we find the same results as in Table 3.1. That is, we continue to find

Table 3.1

**Expected Optimal Retirement Age and Years of Service,
by Entry Age**

	FERS		CSRS	
Entry Age	Age	YOS	Age	YOS
20	55	35	55	35
25	55	30	55	30
30	60	30	60	30
35	60	25	60	25
40	60	20	60	20

that the optimal age-YOS combination for retirement is the same under FERS and under CSRS for individuals who earn more, have steeper pay growth over their careers, and who contribute more to the TSP, given our assumption of an MRA of 55. As before, when the MRA is assumed to be 57, then the optimal retirement age for those who enter at age 20 or 25 is 57 under FERS but 55 under CSRS.

The result that the optimal retirement age-YOS combination is the same under FERS and CSRS also depends crucially on holding entry age or YOS constant in making the comparisons. If this assumption is violated, we find that the retirement age-YOS incentives will differ under the two systems, as shown in Figure 3.2. Suppose we let entry age vary in our comparison of CSRS and FERS. For example, suppose one individual entered at age 40 and was covered by FERS and another individual entered at age 20 and was covered by CSRS. If we compare the maximum expected ACOL values for these individuals, we see that the individual covered by FERS has an incentive to stay longer and retire at age 62, whereas the individual covered by CSRS has an incentive to retire earlier, at age 55.

The reason for the difference in retirement age-YOS incentives is that the two individuals have different years of service at each age. For example, a 50-year-old under FERS has only 10 YOS. A 50-year-old under CSRS has 30 YOS. The 50-year-old under FERS would not even be eligible to retire at age 55 with immediate benefits, unlike the 50-year-old under CSRS. He can retire only as early as age 60, when he has 20 YOS. This example shows the importance of holding YOS, or entry age, constant in comparing retirement age incentives.

This point is important because it helps explain observed differences in retirement ages of those under FERS and under CSRS. Empirically, the average age of retirement is older under FERS, and those under FERS have lower retirement rates (see Chapter Five). The simulation analysis indicates that these differences are not due to different retirement age incentives embedded in these systems. Rather, these comparisons fail to hold YOS constant. Since FERS was only recently implemented, those who retire under FERS tend to have fewer YOS. As shown in Figure 3.2, those with fewer YOS have an incentive to retire later under FERS.

The expected retirement age-YOS incentives discussed so far indicate the age-YOS combination at which an individual at the beginning of his or her career would expect to retire in the future. However, because of nonmonetary or random factors, such as ill health or relatively unpleasant job duties, some individuals will find that

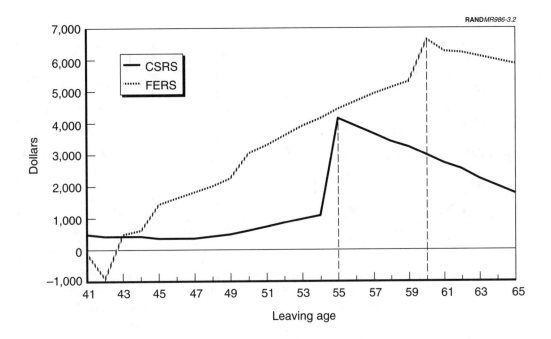

Figure 3.2—ACOL When Entry Age = 20 for CSRS and Entry Age = 40 for FERS

they are better off retiring before, or after, the expected optimal retirement age-YOS combination.

Although it might make sense to retire earlier or later than the optimal retirement age-YOS combination because of nonmonetary factors, those who do will suffer a financial penalty. The financial penalty at each leaving age equals the difference between the expected ACOL at that leaving age and the maximum expected ACOL. At the optimal retirement age-YOS combination, the penalty is zero. Figure 3.3a illustrates the penalty calculation for someone who leaves at age 50 when the maximum ACOL is achieved at age 55. Figure 3.3b graphs the penalty for all leaving or retirement ages beyond age 40.

As Figure 3.3b shows, the simulation model predicts that the penalty for leaving earlier or later than the expected optimal age-YOS combination is lower under FERS. That is, those who leave before the expected optimal retirement age are not as strongly penalized under FERS. Neither are those who retire later than the optimal. Consequently, FERS is predicted to produce more variance in retirement ages than is CSRS, but the average retirement age is predicted to be the same under both systems when the MRA is 55 under FERS. While the penalty for deferring retirement beyond the optimal age-YOS combination is lower under FERS for senior personnel, it is also lower for those who retire earlier. Therefore, this aspect of FERS is not consistent with a prevailing hypothesis regarding FERS.

The penalty is lower under FERS because the path of expected ACOL values ramps up and ramps down more gradually than the one for CSRS. The ramp up is more grad-

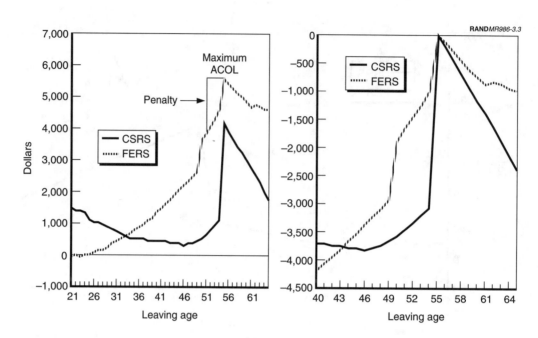

Figure 3.3a—ACOL When Entry Age = 20, Under Both Systems

Figure 3.3b—Penalty from Deviating from Optimal Horizon When Entry Age = 20

ual because of differences in the degree of inflation protection under the two systems and because of differences in the age at which individuals can claim a deferred retirement benefit. Those covered by FERS can claim a deferred annuity as early as age 55. In other words, those who leave before they are eligible for normal retirement, say at age 40, can still claim a FERS retirement benefit at age 55 if they have at least 10 YOS. As the individual ages, the deferred retirement age shifts under FERS. For example, for someone who enters the civil service at age 20, the deferred retirement age shifts from age 62 to age 55 when the individual becomes 30 years old and has 10 YOS. Also, the TSP provides a measure of inflation protection for those who leave before the normal retirement age because those who leave can roll over their TSP into an Individual Retirement Account and continue to earn an average rate of return that tends to protect their fund from inflation.

Under CSRS, a deferred annuity can be claimed only at age 62. The expected ACOL rises dramatically at age 55 under CSRS because once the individual becomes eligible for normal retirement benefits, the discounting of the retirement benefit shifts from age 62 to age 55, and the payout of benefits is for a longer period. Also, the retirement annuity for which the employee is eligible is not inflation protected if he or she leaves prior to being eligible for normal retirement. Both of these factors lower the expected ACOL under CSRS for every leaving age prior to age 55, as shown in Figure 3.3a.

Beyond the optimal retirement age, the expected ACOL also falls more gradually under FERS. Deferring retirement beyond the optimal age results in a smaller expected ACOL because the annuity is paid out for a shorter period of time. However, the expected ACOL is larger because the employee's retirement annuity increases with earnings and YOS. The size of the penalty associated with deferring retirement beyond the optimal age depends on the relative size of these factors. For someone who enters the civil service at age 20, pay growth beyond age 55 is generally quite small. Therefore, the growth in the retirement annuity for those covered by CSRS and FERS is also generally quite small. However, FERS has an extra advantage for those who defer retirement. They get another year's worth of contributions (including government matching contributions) to their TSP fund. As a result, the gain to deferring retirement is higher under FERS, implying that the overall net penalty from doing so is lower.

SEPARATION INCENTIVES

Another hypothesis regarding FERS was that it provides stronger incentives to leave among mid- and late-career personnel. As discussed in Chapter Two, to determine whether separation incentives are stronger or weaker under FERS compared with those under CSRS, we simulate the maximum expected ACOL values at each decision age under each system. The system that has higher maximum expected ACOL values at each decision age has weaker separation incentives and the stronger stay incentives.

The results of our simulations for an individual who enters at age 20 are shown in Figure 3.4. The path of maximized expected ACOL values for FERS crosses the path for CSRS. For those in early and mid-career, the FERS path is somewhat higher than the CSRS path is. For those in late career, the FERS path is lower. Consequently, the net gain to staying (or the cost of leaving) is somewhat greater under FERS in the

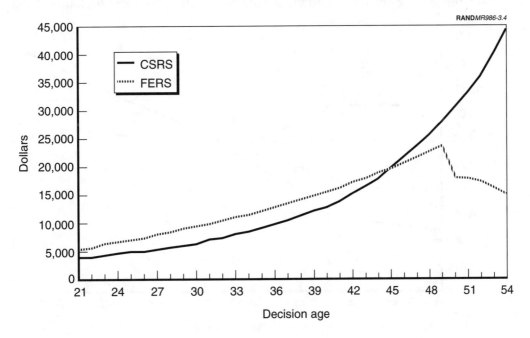

Figure 3.4—Maximum Expected ACOL by Decision Age When Entry Age = 20

early and mid-career years, but smaller in the later years. In other words, we find that stay incentives are stronger under FERS in the early and mid-career but weaker in the late-career years. We find similar results for older entrants (see Figure 3.5).

The implication of this result is that, all else equal, we would expect turnover rates for mid-career personnel to be somewhat lower under FERS but higher for those nearing retirement age. This result is partially but not entirely consistent with the intent of FERS.

The main reason why turnover incentives are weaker under FERS for early and mid-careerists is that FERS is a more generous retirement system. Consequently, an individual has more to lose by not staying and accumulating an even larger benefit under this system. Although individuals who separate can continue to earn an inflation-protected rate of return on their TSP accumulations, the net value of staying in the civil service and continuing to make contributions to the fund make it more worthwhile to stay in the civil service than to leave.

To illustrate the role played by the relative generosity of FERS benefits in affecting the relative turnover incentives under FERS compared with those under CSRS, we arbitrarily redefined FERS to make it less generous and simulated the maximum expected ACOL values at each decision age under this redefined system. We then compared the new path of maximum expected ACOL values under FERS with the path for CSRS.

We could have chosen a variety of ways to make FERS a less generous system. For simplicity, we eliminated the Basic (defined benefit) Plan under FERS. Instead, we considered what would happen to the maximized ACOL values, and therefore to the

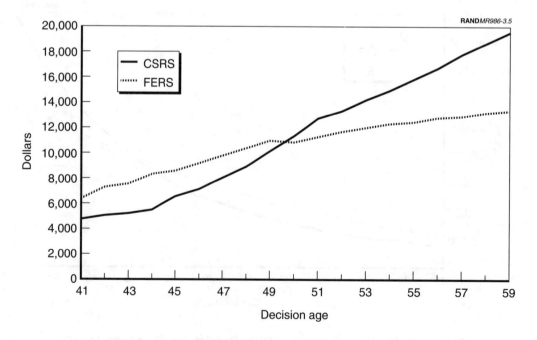

Figure 3.5—Maximum Expected ACOL by Decision Age When Entry Age = 40

relative turnover incentives under FERS and CSRS, if FERS consisted of only Social Security and the Thrift Savings Plan. Eliminating the Basic Plan would obviously make the FERS retirement benefit less generous.

We find that when FERS is defined to be a less generous system, stay incentives in the early and mid-career are weaker under FERS than under CSRS, just the opposite of the earlier result.

We illustrate the path of maximum expected ACOL values under the redefined FERS and under CSRS in Figure 3.6 for someone who entered the civil service at age 20. The redefined FERS path now lies entirely below the CSRS path, indicating that separation incentives are uniformly stronger under FERS when FERS is redefined to be a less generous system.

In sum, we find that turnover incentives among junior and mid-career civil service personnel are actually weaker under FERS, contrary to earlier suggestions regarding the turnover incentives produced by FERS. If FERS offered less generous benefits, we find that turnover incentives would be stronger under FERS for these individuals. On the other hand, consistent with earlier suggestions, FERS turnover incentives are stronger for those nearing retirement. Past research (Asch and Warner, 1994) shows that greater turnover in the more senior grades provides promotion opportunities and effort incentives for those in the junior grades. Furthermore, greater turnover overall provides opportunities to rejuvenate the force. It is unclear whether the reduced turnover incentives of the mid-career force offsets the greater turnover incentives of the senior force to create more promotion opportunities for junior personnel.

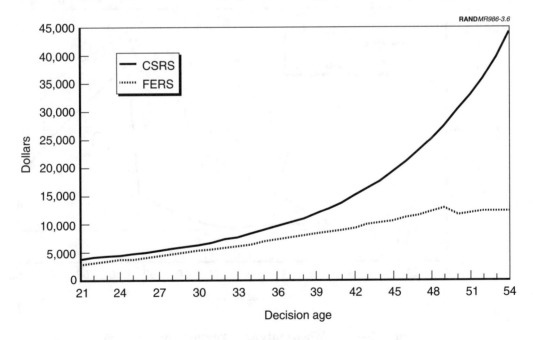

Figure 3.6—Maximum Expected ACOL by Decision Age for FERS Without the Basic Plan When Entry Age = 20

In Chapter Six, we compare separation rates under FERS and CSRS for mid-careerists to determine whether we can detect empirical differences in addition to theoretical ones.

INCENTIVES TO SWITCH TO FERS

We also used our simulation model to examine the incentives to switch to FERS from CSRS, all else equal. We first simulate the expected ACOL values (ACOL(N,1)) for someone who spends an entire career under CSRS. We then compare these to the values for someone who is covered by CSRS until the switch age and then is covered by FERS thereafter. If the path of expected ACOL values is higher under the latter path, the individual's expected lifetime net earnings and retirement wealth at each leaving age is higher by switching to FERS. Of particular interest is the comparison of the maximum ACOL values. If the maximum expected ACOL value is higher, the individual's expected maximum net earnings and retirement wealth at the optimal retirement age-YOS combination will be higher if he or she switches to FERS. We conduct these simulations for different switch ages.[3]

The main result is that individuals who face the switch decision early in their careers are better off financially by switching to FERS, all else equal. The comparison of the path of expected ACOL values for young entrants (age 20) who face the switch decision when they have five years of service is shown in Figure 3.7. The path of expected ACOL values is uniformly higher beyond the FERS vesting point for those who switch

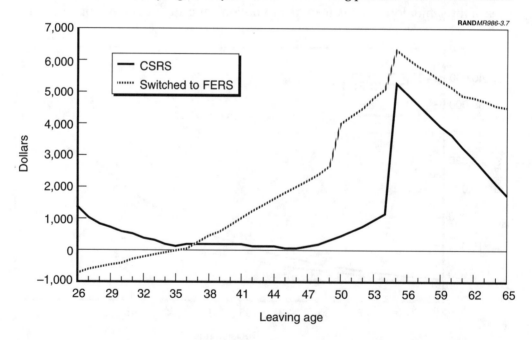

Figure 3.7—ACOL When Entry Age = 20 and Switch Age = 25

---

[3]We also conduct the simulations for different entry ages. Since the qualitative results are similar to those discussed in the text, the results of these simulations are not shown.

than for those who do not. Importantly, the expected maximum ACOL is higher for the individuals who switch. Consequently, expected lifetime net earnings and retirement wealth is higher at the optimal retirement point.

For individuals who face the switch decision later in their careers, the simulation model predicts that they are better off financially by remaining under CSRS if they expect to stay in the civil service until they retire. Figure 3.8 shows the path of expected ACOL values for individuals who enter the civil service at age 20 and face the switch decision at age 40. The paths cross over at age 55. At and beyond age 55 (until age 64), the expected ACOL values at each leaving age are higher for individuals who stay under CSRS than for those who switch to FERS. Individuals are predicted to maximize their expected net lifetime earnings and retirement wealth at age 55, the optimal retirement point, by staying under CSRS. They are better off by remaining under CSRS because those who start FERS later in their careers have fewer years in which to grow their TSP accumulations. In addition, CSRS retirement benefits increase with YOS in a nonlinear fashion because the multiplier in the benefits formula rises with YOS. As a result, individuals with more YOS under CSRS have more to lose by switching to FERS, all else equal.

However, before age 55, the expected ACOL values are higher for individuals who switch to FERS. The model predicts that those who do not expect to remain until the optimal retirement age, say because of nonmonetary factors, will be better off by

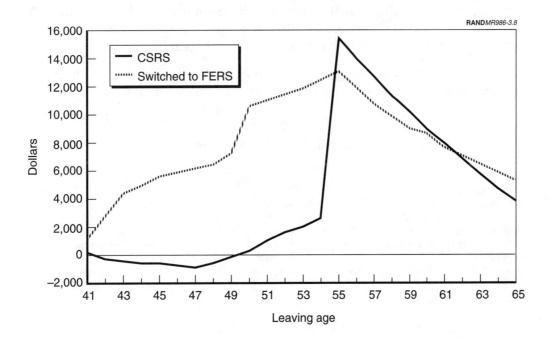

Figure 3.8—ACOL When Entry Age = 20 and Switch Age = 40

switching to FERS. Therefore, whether individuals facing the decision to switch to FERS in mid- and late career should switch depends on their career expectations.[4]

SENSITIVITY ANALYSES

As discussed in Chapter Two, our simulation analyses are based on a series of assumptions. To determine how sensitive our results are to these assumptions, we conducted a variety of sensitivity analyses. The second column in Table 3.2 lists the assumptions we made in deriving the results we have presented so far. The third column indicates how we varied each assumption. Specifically, we examine how our results change when we assume, alternatively, a higher inflation rate, a higher minimum retirement age, a higher personnel discount rate, a higher TSP growth rate, a higher TSP employee contribution rate, and a higher and steeper pay profile. Since the Balanced Budget Act of 1997 increased employee contribution rates temporarily for CSRS and the FERS Basic Plan, we also examine how our results would change when the employee contribution rate is 7.5 percent under CSRS and 1.3 percent under the FERS Basic Plan.[5] Finally, we assume a somewhat different pay profile in the alternative sector than in the base case. The base case assumes that the individual will exit the labor force at age 65. That is, an individual who retires from the civil service at, say, age 55, is assumed to find a job for 10 years in the alternative sector in the base case. In the sensitivity analysis, we alter this assumption and assume that the individual who retires from the civil service also exits from the labor force. Using the example, the sensitivity analysis assumes that an individual who retires from the civil service at age 55 would also exit the labor force at age 55 and therefore would have zero earnings in the alternative sector for those 10 years.

The variations we make are somewhat arbitrary in some cases. We tried to choose assumptions that reasonably spanned the set of feasible alternatives. For example,

Table 3.2

Assumptions That We Varied

Assumption	Base Case	Variations
Inflation rate	3 percent	6 percent
Minimum retirement age	age 55	age 57
Personal discount rate (PDR)	5 percent	10 percent
TSP average growth rate	6 percent	15 percent
TSP employee contribution rate	varies with age	5 percent for all ages
Pay profile	median	high
Contribution rates under CSRS, Basic Plan	7.0 percent, 0.8 percent	7.5 percent, 1.3 percent
Alternative pay profile	Exit at age 65	Exit at C.S. retirement age

NOTE: C.S. = civil service.

---

[4]Other factors may affect the decision to switch, such as expectations about future returns. Even individuals facing the switch decision early in their careers may not switch if they expect a low return, or even a loss, on their accumulations. Such expectations might explain why relatively few individuals switched during the open period in 1988, because it closely followed the stock market's "Black Monday" in October 1987. Nonetheless, the simulation model predicts, all else equal, that those facing the switch decision earlier in their careers are more likely to switch than those facing it later.

[5]This temporary change is discussed in Appendix A.

given the low rates of inflation experienced in recent years, an average rate of inflation between 3 percent and 6 percent seemed to span the range the employee might expect over an entire lifetime. We consider a minimum retirement age of 57 since this is the MRA that applies to those born after 1970, and therefore to most young entrants to the civil service in recent years. We consider a higher contribution rate to the TSP, equal to 5 percent, to reflect the growth in contribution rates in recent years. The alternative pay profile we consider is for someone who obtains more education and enters the civil service at a later age but at a higher level of pay and who experiences more wage growth than the individual in the base case. This higher pay profile is the same one we used to examine how retirement results would change for those in senior leadership positions, discussed earlier in this chapter.

We varied these assumptions individually. For example, when we ran the simulation model under the higher-pay profile assumption, we maintained the other assumptions. However, the assumptions are correlated. For example, available evidence indicates that those who earn more also contribute a higher fraction of their earnings to their TSP (see Thrift Savings Plan Board, 1997). In addition, those who earn more may earn a higher rate of return on their TSP fund because they have a greater incentive to learn about investment options. An alternative way to conduct the sensitivity analyses would be to vary the assumptions jointly. Because our sensitivity analysis does not do this, it provides only a partial view of how our results would change under alternative scenarios.

Table 3.3 summarizes the results of the sensitivity analyses. The first column lists the various assumptions. Columns (2) through (5) indicate the main results we found earlier and correspond to the titles of the earlier subsections. Column (2) refers to our earlier result that found that FERS is a relatively more generous system. Column (3) refers to our result that retirement age-YOS incentives are the same under CSRS and FERS. Column (4) refers to our result that separation incentives are somewhat weaker under FERS for those in their early and mid-careers. Column (5) refers to the result that those who face a switch decision early in their careers are better off financially if they switch to FERS. An "X" in one of the columns in Table 3.3 indicates that the main result found earlier was reversed or changed in some major way when the assumption was varied. If there is no "X" the quantitative results may still have changed, but the results were not reversed.

For example, when we assumed a higher rate of inflation, the expected ACOL values at each leaving age under FERS compared with those under CSRS changed. Nonetheless, we continued to find the same general results as before. Therefore, no "X" appears in the first row of Table 3.3. As another example, when we assume that individuals who retire from the civil service also exit the labor force, we find that the optimal retirement age is as late as possible. That is, we find that individuals always increase their lifetime wealth by working another year in the government. However, we find the same result under FERS and under CSRS, so our overall conclusions regarding our comparison of FERS and CSRS are the same in Table 3.3.

When we assume a higher minimum retirement age under FERS, we find that the optimal retirement age under FERS for young entrants became 57 instead of age 55,

Table 3.3

Results of Sensitivity Analyses
(X indicates a change from the base case result)

Assumption (1)	Relative Generosity (2)	Retirement Age Incentives (3)	Separation Incentives (4)	Incentives to Switch to FERS (5)
Inflation rate				
MRA		X		
PDR	X			X
TSP growth rate		X		
TSP contribution rate				X
Pay profile				X
TSP growth rate		X		
Contribution rate to CSRS, Basic Plan				
Alt. pay profile				

the optimal under CSRS. Therefore, recent (young) entrants to the civil service who are covered by FERS are predicted to retire at later ages than they would have retired had they been covered by CSRS instead.

When we assume a higher personal discount rate (PDR), we find that CSRS is the more generous system. The reason is that individuals contribute more of their earnings to FERS than they do to CSRS. These contributions are deducted from current pay. Although retirement benefits are also more generous under FERS, these benefits are not realized until later in the employee's lifetime.

When the discount rate is higher, the discounted present value of these future benefits are smaller. Consequently, FERS seems less generous.

Interestingly, we find only one major change in the results when we assume a significantly greater TSP rate of return. Individuals covered by FERS have an incentive to retire later than those covered by CSRS. The reason is that individuals who leave earlier forgo the opportunity to continue accumulating and receiving matching contributions to their TSP fund. We also find that most of the results are the same when we assume a higher pay profile. However, because we do not vary other assumptions, such as the TSP contribution rates, when we vary the pay assumption, these particular sensitivity results may not be realistic.

DATA AND EMPIRICAL APPROACH

The empirical analysis focuses on how separation outcomes in the early and mid-career of civil service employees differ for those under FERS compared with those under CSRS. A key result of the simulation analysis in Chapter Three is that FERS embeds weaker separation incentives for those in their early and mid-careers. The goal of the empirical analysis is to examine whether actual separation rates are predicted to be lower for those covered by FERS. In this chapter, we describe the data set we use, some confounding factors in the data analysis, and our empirical approach. The next chapter presents the empirical results.

We examine separation rather than retirement outcomes empirically because no one in the civil service has spent an entire career and retired under FERS. Given that only those who entered since 1984 are covered by FERS, insufficient time has passed. It would be possible to compare the retirement rates of those who spent only a partial career under FERS and under CSRS, but relatively few people have either retired under FERS or have spent a partial career under CSRS.[1] In addition, one would need to address possible selection biases that arise from the possibility that those who spend a partial career under FERS or CSRS and retire are not a random group of civil service personnel. Later in this chapter we will discuss how the lack of time under FERS and the implementation of FERS creates some confounding factors in our analysis of separation outcomes.

DATA

The data we used are beginning-fiscal-year inventories of DoD civil service personnel from FY82 to FY96 provided by the Defense Manpower Data Center. We limited our data analysis to a subsample of the population. We excluded from the analysis file those individuals who were temporary workers, worked less than full-time, were considered "inactive" employees, or were seasonal. We excluded these individuals because they may have less attachment to the labor force, have higher separation rates, and be disproportionately represented among those covered by FERS. Including them could bias our analysis of separation rates under the two systems. We also

---

[1] Relatively few individuals switched to FERS in the 1980s. For example, in the first FERS transfer program in 1987, the General Accounting Office found only 4 percent switched to FERS (GAO, 1998). Consequently, relatively few individuals are in their late career and covered by FERS.

excluded military technicians because they are covered by a different FERS plan specifically designed for them and because they serve in a uniformed military component as well.[2] Overall, about 20 percent of each annual inventory was deleted. Figure 4.1 shows the total size of the inventory in each year and the inventory size in each year after we made these exclusions.

Given the enormous size of each inventory, even after the exclusions were made, and the amount of time it takes to process these data, we chose to work with a 20 percent random subsample stratified by year. In other words, we randomly selected 20 percent of each annual inventory and merged the subsamples to form one data set. Sampling cuts the size of the data set, net of exclusions, from 12,427,967 observations to 2,485,593.

The data include a wide range of information on each individual including various job characteristics and individual characteristics. The job characteristics include information on occupational area, component (e.g., Army, Navy, Air Force, Marines, or defense agency), pay plan (e.g., general schedule or wage grade), grade, years of service, last performance rating, and supervisor or managerial status. By matching inventories across years, we can determine whether an individual entered the DoD civil service in the past year.[3] By determining which individuals are in the current inventory but were not in the previous year's inventory, we can indicate which individuals were part of the inflow into the annual DoD inventory.[4] The individual characteristics include gender, race and ethnicity, education,[5] region, veteran's status, retirement system coverage (e.g., FERS or CSRS), reported handicap status, age, and whether the individual switched to FERS.[6]

---

[2]As will be discussed later in the text, our analysis will also exclude those covered by other retirement plans, such as CSRS-Offset and CSRS-Interim.

[3]The inventories were matched before the 20 percent random samples were drawn.

[4]The data do not permit easy identification of new hires versus rehires. First, the YOS variable in our data set includes active duty military service. Consequently, an individual may be a new hire to the civil service but enter with YOS greater than one, indicating that the individual is a veteran. Second, some individuals appear to be rehires or transfers from another federal agency because their YOS are greater than zero at entry and they are not veterans. Yet, these individuals never appear in one of our earlier inventory files. While long gaps in civil service are possible, it is also possible that these individuals are really new hires with a miscoded YOS variable. As discussed later in the text, the YOS variable was somewhat problematic in our data set.

[5]The education variable is also problematic in our data set. According to the Defense Manpower Data Center, the education variable in the data set is not always updated when an individual accumulates more education. Nonetheless, the education variable should accurately reflect entry education. Insofar as most individuals do not significantly increase their education over their careers, it is not clear how much of a problem the lack of updating is. Even if many do significantly increase their education over their careers, entry education should provide some control for how separation rates vary by education level. As discussed later in the text, we conduct sensitivity analysis to examine how sensitive our empirical results are to inclusion or exclusion of this variable.

[6]We identify each individual's retirement system coverage using the variable in the data set indicating retirement system. We also checked the years of service variable and fiscal year variable to make sure individuals were not incorrectly coded as being covered by FERS or by CSRS. Individuals for whom system coverage was clearly incorrect were deleted from the data set; however, few observations had this problem. Still, because some individuals were assigned to the wrong retirement system by their agency, our data may indicate an incorrect retirement system for those cases. (See Causer, 1998.)

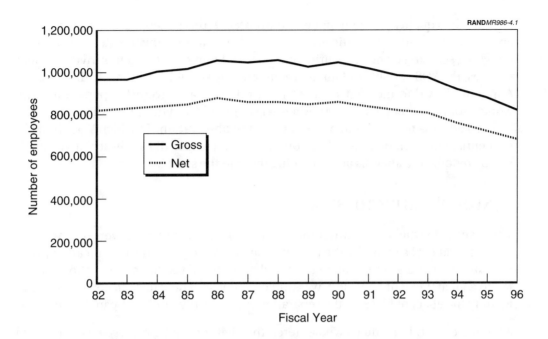

Figure 4.1—Size of Annual Inventories Before and After Exclusions

A key variable in our analysis is whether an individual who was in the beginning-fis-cal-year inventory separated during the fiscal year. To construct this variable we matched the annual inventories to determine which individuals in a given fiscal year inventory were no longer in the inventory in the following year. We called these exits. To determine whether the exit was a separation or a retirement, we made use of transaction data provided by the Defense Manpower Data Center. A transaction record is generated whenever an individual leaves the DoD civil service. The transaction record indicates the type of exit that occurred, e.g., involuntary separation, voluntary retirement, and so forth. We consider an exit to be a separation if the individual had a transaction record indicating that a separation occurred. Since there is a nontrivial number of cases in which an exit occurs but there is no transaction record indicating the type of exit, we conducted sensitivity analysis with our definition of separation, including adding the indeterminate exits to the known cases of separations.

One potential problem with our definition of separations is that it is defined relative to DoD and not relative to the civil service. For example, individuals may leave the DoD civil service to work in another civil service agency, such as the Department of Energy. These individuals will appear as separations in our data set. Yet, individuals who transfer between civil service agencies are usually covered by the same retirement system. Technically speaking, the data include a variable that indicates whether the individual is a transfer to or from another civil service agency. However, this variable is highly error-ridden according to the Defense Manpower Data Center. Therefore, our data do not allow us to distinguish accurately between transfers to another agency and separations from the civil service.

Another data quality problem that we confronted in this analysis is that the YOS variable is problematic. Specifically, we linked the annual inventories together by matching scrambled Social Security numbers and found that, in a nontrivial number of cases, the YOS variable did not increment in any sensible fashion. As discussed in Appendix B, we found that most of the problem cases were for personnel who worked for the Air Force in the Air Materiel Command and for those who were veterans. To address this problem, we identified the observations in which YOS were not sequential and excluded them from our analysis. We also did some sensitivity analysis by redoing the analysis and including them in the sample.

CONFOUNDING FACTORS

The manner in which FERS was implemented and the fact that it covers only workers who entered civil service for the first time since 1984 create an "identification problem" in our analysis of separation rates under FERS and CSRS. In this section, we detail to a greater extent how FERS was implemented and how this affects our ability to identify the effect of FERS on the separation rates of early- and mid-career personnel.

As noted earlier, individuals who entered the civil service before 1984 were covered by CSRS. In 1984, it became clear that a new retirement system would be introduced, but the specifics of the new plan had not been determined. Therefore, beginning in 1984, those who entered the civil service were no longer placed under CSRS but, instead, were placed under a plan called CSRS-Interim. This interim system included both CSRS and Social Security coverage. In 1987, when FERS was introduced, new entrants since 1984 were placed automatically under FERS. Reentrants (e.g., those who were rehired after 1984 but were originally covered by CSRS) were also automatically placed under FERS if they had fewer than five YOS. Reentrants with more than five YOS had the option of joining CSRS-Offset, the new name for the CSRS-Interim plan. Existing CSRS-covered employees had the option of switching to FERS between 1987 and 1988. In July 1988, the switching window was closed. It was opened again in July 1998 for six months.

Figure 4.2 shows the fraction of civil service personnel in each annual inventory that is covered by CSRS, CSRS-Interim/Offset, or FERS. FERS coverage rose from about 20 percent in FY88, the first year for which we have data on FERS, to about 50 percent in FY96. Coverage rose as more individuals entered the civil service over time under FERS and as more individuals under CSRS retired or separated.

Because of the way FERS was implemented, e.g., grandfathering existing employees under CSRS with some switching allowed and automatically covering new employees under FERS, the age and YOS distributions of those under FERS and those under CSRS differ markedly. The age distributions for all years in our data set are shown in Figure 4.3, and the YOS distributions are shown in Figure 4.4. Those under FERS are considerably younger and have fewer YOS. For example, the mean YOS in the sample is 17.4 for those under CSRS but is 7.2 for those under FERS. These differences have gotten even starker over time as shown in Figures 4.5 and 4.6 for FY96. For ex-

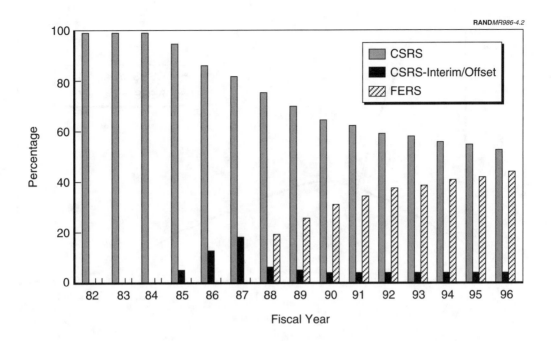

Figure 4.2—Fraction of DoD Civil Service Personnel Under CSRS, FERS, and CSRS-Interim/Offset

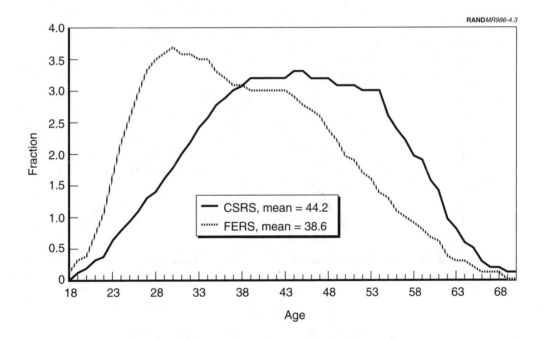

Figure 4.3—Age Distribution for Both Systems, All Years

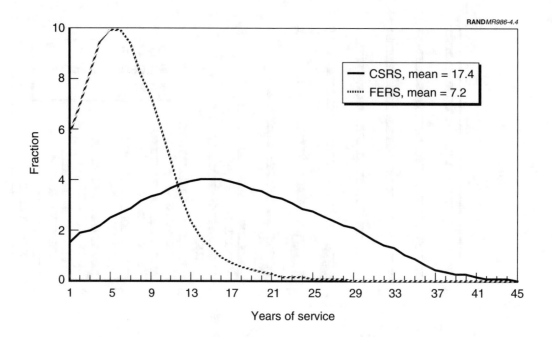

Figure 4.4—YOS Distribution for Both Systems, All Years

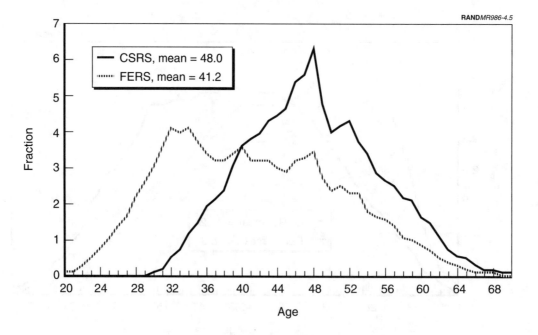

Figure 4.5—Age Distribution for Both Systems, FY96

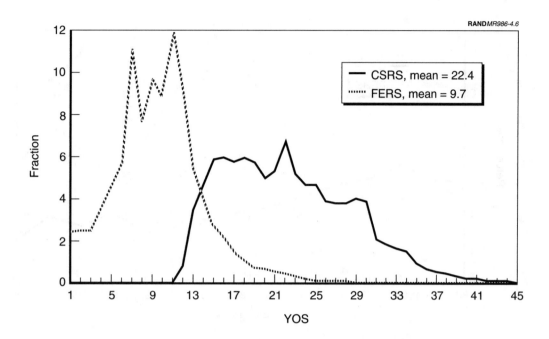

Figure 4.6—YOS Distribution for Both Systems, FY96

ample, the average YOS in FY96 of those covered by FERS was 9.7, while it was 22.4 for those covered by CSRS.[7]

These differences in the age and YOS distributions of those covered by FERS compared with those by CSRS have implications for our analysis of separation rates. Figure 4.7 shows mean separation rates by year for those covered by CSRS and those covered by FERS. Figure 4.8 shows mean retirement rates by year by retirement system coverage. We find that those covered by FERS have higher average separation rates and lower average retirement rates. However, since younger and more-junior civil service personnel are more likely to separate and less likely to retire in general, those covered by FERS may have higher separation rates and lower retirement rates because of their youth and lack of experience.

This suggests a need to control for age and YOS in our comparisons of separation rates between those covered by FERS and those covered by CSRS. In Figure 4.9 we show mean separation rates by age in FY96. Even controlling for age, we continue to find that those covered by FERS have higher separation rates. In fact, based on the comparison in Figure 4.9, one would conclude that FERS embeds stronger turnover incentives than CSRS for those in their mid-careers. This would be contrary to what our simulation model predicted in Chapter Three. However, the comparison in Figure 4.9 does not control for YOS.

_____

[7]The difference in mean age of those covered by FERS versus those covered by CSRS is less stark in FY96 (Figure 4.5) than in all years combined (Figure 4.3) because the average age of new hires has risen over time in the civil service and the DoD civilian workforce has gotten considerably older overall.

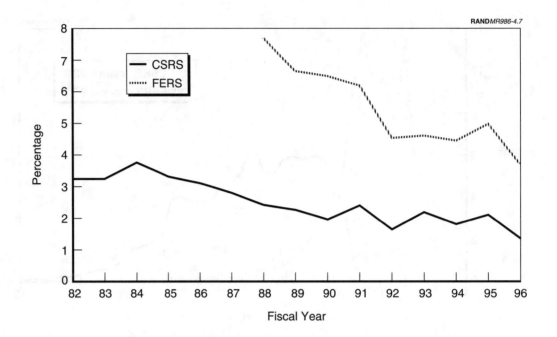

Figure 4.7—Mean Separation Rates by Year for Both Systems

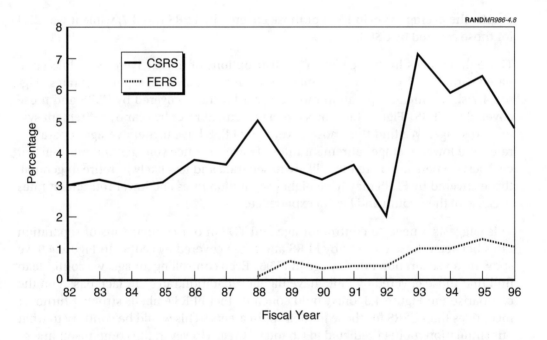

Figure 4.8—Mean Retirement Rates by Year for Both Systems

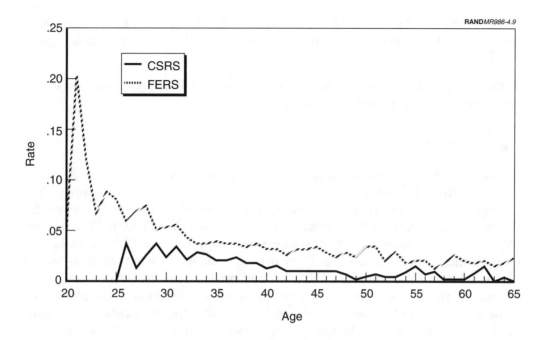

Figure 4.9—Mean Separation Rates by Age for Both Systems, FY96

Because of the way FERS was implemented, controlling for age, YOS, *and* fiscal year in comparisons of separation rates of those covered by FERS and CSRS is not straightforward. As Figures 4.5 and 4.6 suggest, relatively few individuals who are covered by CSRS are junior enough and relatively few individuals who are covered by FERS are senior enough to be compared with one another in a recent fiscal year. If we exclude those covered by CSRS-Offset, all personnel covered by CSRS in FY96 have at least 12 YOS. If we exclude those who switched to FERS voluntarily, all personnel covered by FERS in FY96 have at most 12 YOS.

Because some switching was allowed in 1987 and 1988, not everyone covered by FERS was automatically placed under this system. If those who chose to switch have characteristics, unrelated to the incentives embedded in FERS, that make them more likely to separate from the civil service, then including them in our analysis could bias our comparison of separation rates under FERS and CSRS. Consequently, we exclude these individuals from our analysis. Excluding these observations exacerbates the problem associated with identifying the effect of FERS on separation rates discussed in the previous paragraph. Only those who switched to FERS have enough YOS or are old enough to be compared with CSRS personnel of similar ages and YOS in a given fiscal year.

For similar reasons, we exclude those covered by CSRS-Interim/Offset from our analysis. Individuals who left the civil service and returned might have characteristics unrelated to the incentives embedded in CSRS that make them more or less likely to separate. Furthermore, their behavior might be affected by their Social Security coverage. Including these personnel could bias our comparison of separation rates under FERS and CSRS. However, excluding these personnel exacerbates the identification problem because these personnel are likely to be the only individuals under CSRS who have few enough YOS to be compared with those under FERS in a given fiscal year.

In the next section, we discuss our empirical approach and specifically how we attempt to address the identification problem.

EMPIRICAL APPROACH

To address the identification problem, we compare the early- and mid-career separation outcomes of those under FERS in the later fiscal years in our sample, FY89 through FY96, to those of early- and mid-career personnel under CSRS in an early fiscal year in our sample, FY83. In FY83 no one was covered by FERS.[8] In FY89 through FY96, our data include individuals who were covered by either CSRS or FERS. We exclude the years FY84 through FY88 because our data do not indicate which personnel were either covered by FERS or had switched to FERS from CSRS. As an example of the approach, we compare the separation rates among individuals with 12 or fewer YOS in FY96 who are covered by FERS with the separation rates among individuals with 12 or fewer YOS in FY83 who are covered by CSRS. We chose 12 YOS as the cutoff YOS for FY96 because only those who entered since 1984 were automatically covered by FERS.

Of course, any difference in the separation rates of those covered by CSRS in the early 1980s and those covered by FERS in the late 1980s and early 1990s could be unrelated to differences in retirement system coverage and be related to general environmental changes that occurred between these years. For example, individuals in the 1990s may have viewed their career prospective differently in light of the drawdown in the DoD civil service that occurred in 1992 and 1993 and changed their separation behavior relative to individuals in the early 1980s.

To address this issue, we needed to create a control group, namely a group of early- and mid-career civil service personnel who were present in both in the early 1980s and in the late 1980s and early 1990s and who were covered by the same retirement system. Such a control group would allow us to net out differences in separation rates due to differences in fiscal year from our comparison of separation rates under FERS and CSRS. Unfortunately, no such control group exists.

We proxy the control group with a group of senior personnel who were under CSRS in both the early 1980s and the late 1980s and early 1990s. For example, we compare the separation rates among individuals with 24 YOS who were covered by CSRS in FY89 with the separation rates among individuals with 24 YOS who were covered by CSRS in FY83 . We assume that any difference in the separation rates between these two groups captures differences related to changes in the general environment be-

---

[8]We do not use FY82 because several variables are missing or do not vary in this inventory, such as geographic region and performance rating. For sensitivity analysis, we rerun the regression using data from FY82 and FY83 but excluding those variables that had missing values or no variation in FY82. We find that our main results are unchanged.

tween these two periods. To identify the effect of FERS on separation rates, we subtract the difference in separation rates in the control group from the difference in separation rates among junior and mid-career civil service personnel covered by FERS compared with those covered by CSRS.

For our proxy control group to be meaningful, we must assume that the effect of environmental changes on separation rates is the same for senior as it is for junior and mid-career personnel. This assumption may be questionable. However, this is the only alternative available. When making major changes to the retirement system in the future, Congress should consider initiating a test concurrent with or prior to the policy change that would create a control group, allowing identification of the effect of the policy.

As discussed previously, our analysis excludes all individuals who were voluntarily switched to FERS. We exclude them from the analysis in two ways. First, we use the variable in the data set indicating a switch to FERS to delete all personnel in the data for whom this variable indicated a switch. Second, we selected personnel on the basis of their YOS. In FY96, we selected only individuals covered by FERS who had 12 or fewer YOS. Since only those entering since 1984 could be automatically covered by FERS, only those with 12 or fewer YOS in FY96 were automatically placed under FERS. In FY95, we selected individuals covered by FERS who had 11 or fewer YOS, and so forth. Finally, for FY89, we selected individuals covered by FERS who had five or fewer YOS. Table 4.1 lists, by fiscal year, the individual covered by FERS who we included in our analysis sample. We compare the separation rates of these individuals with individuals covered by CSRS who have 12 or fewer YOS in FY83. This selection of CSRS personnel in FY83 is also shown in Table 4.1.

Because we use senior personnel covered by CSRS to proxy the control group in our analysis, we needed to include only those senior individuals covered by CSRS who had no incentive to switch to FERS during the open switching period in 1987 and 1988. Otherwise, our group of individuals covered by CSRS would be self-selected, and their presence could introduce a selectivity bias into our analysis. Empirically, we found that no one with 24 YOS or more in FY89 switched to FERS. In our analysis of switching incentives in Chapter Two, we found that individuals who face a switch decision late in their careers have no incentive to switch. Therefore, to form the control group, we chose those individuals covered by CSRS who had 24 or more YOS in FY89, who had 25 or more YOS in FY90, and so forth. In FY96, we chose individuals covered by CSRS who had 31 or more YOS. The selection of CSRS personnel by YOS is also shown in Table 4.1.

Figures 4.10 and 4.11 illustrate an example of the basic approach we use to estimate the effect of FERS on separation rates. As Figure 4.10 shows, we compare the separation rates by age of those with 12 or fewer YOS in FY96 and covered by FERS to the rates by age of those with 12 or fewer YOS in FY83 who were covered by CSRS. In this example, the rates are quite close. Because this comparison might reflect differences in separation rates that are due to changes that occurred in the general environment between FY96 and FY83, we compare the rates in Figure 4.10 to the difference in rates among the control group. The rates for the control group in each fiscal year are

Table 4.1

Years of Service Sample Selection

Fiscal Year	Covered by FERS	Covered by CSRS
83	—	YOS ≤ 12, YOS ≥ 24
89	YOS ≤ 5	YOS ≥ 24
90	YOS ≤ 6	YOS ≥ 25
91	YOS ≤ 7	YOS ≥ 26
92	YOS ≤ 8	YOS ≥ 27
93	YOS ≤ 9	YOS ≥ 28
94	YOS ≤ 10	YOS ≥ 29
95	YOS ≤ 11	YOS ≥ 30
96	YOS ≤ 12	YOS ≥ 31

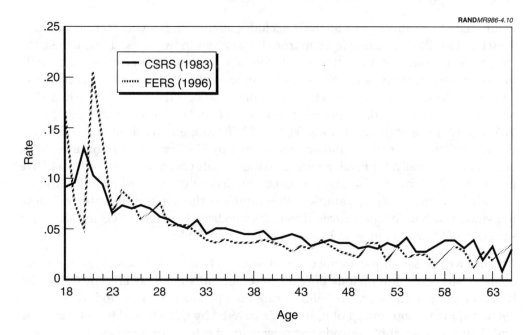

**Figure 4.10—Separation Rates by Age When YOS ≤12
(CSRS in FY83 and FERS in FY96)**

shown in Figure 4.11. As the figure indicates, the separation rates of those covered by CSRS with 31 or more YOS in FY83 are similar to the ones in FY96.

Because factors other than retirement system or fiscal year can affect separation outcomes, we estimate a reduced form logit model that allows us to control for the effect of some of these other factors. In the logit model, the probability of separating is modeled as a function of a set of covariates where the probability density function is the logistic distribution that we denote as G. The model we estimate is of the following form:

$$\Pr ob(S_{it} = 1) = G(a + bF_{it} + cX_{it})$$
$$= \exp[a + bF_{it} + cX_{it}]/\{1 + \exp[a + bF_{it} + cX_{it}]\}.$$

(4.1)

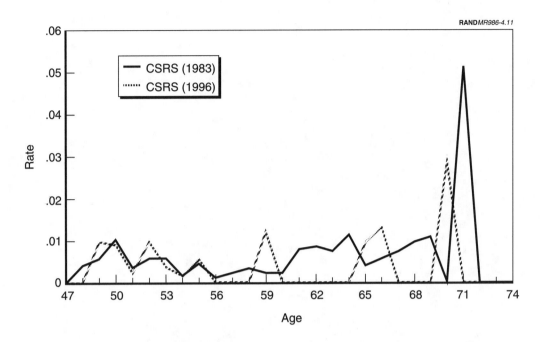

**Figure 4.11—Separation Rates by Age When YOS ≥ 31
(CSRS in FY83 and CSRS in FY96)**

S_{it} equals one if individual i separated in fiscal year t and is equal to zero if he or she did not. The variable F_{it} represents FERS coverage. If individual i is covered by FERS at time t, the F_{it} equals one; otherwise it equals zero. The individual's personal and job characteristics are represented by X_{it}; a, b, and c are parameters that we estimate. The definition of the variables included in X_{it} and their means are given in Appendix C.

Because we are particularly interested in how FERS affects separation rates for mid-career personnel, we estimate a model that allows the effect of FERS on separation rates to vary by age. Specifically, the model we estimate is

$$\mathrm{Prob}(S_{it} = 1) = G[a + b_1 F_{it} + b_2 (F_{it} \times A_{it}) + cX_{it}]. \tag{4.2}$$

The variables represented by A_{it} are indicators of the individual's age group. The estimated effect of FERS on separation rates will equal $G(a^* + b^*_1 + b^*_2 A^*_{it} + cX^*_{it}) - G(a^* + cX^*_{it})$, where a^*, b^*_1, and b^*_2 are parameter estimates of a, b_1, and b_2, respectively. A^*_{it} represents the mean values of A_{it}, and X^*_{it} represents the mean values of the variables included in X_{it}. The estimated effect of FERS on separation rates for individuals in a given age group will be $G(a^* + b^*_1 + b^*_{2j} + cX^*_{it}) - G(a^* + cX^*_{it})$, where j indicates the age group of interest.

We present the results of our empirical analysis in the next chapter.

Chapter Five

EMPIRICAL ANALYSIS OF MID-CAREER SEPARATION RATES

This chapter presents the results of our analysis of separation rates of junior and mid-career civil service personnel under FERS and those under CSRS. As discussed in Chapter Four, we use data on DoD civilian personnel from FY83 and from FY89–FY96 to estimate Eq. (4.2).

Table 5.1 presents the coefficient estimates for the variables of interest, the FERS variables and the age variables. The full regression results are reported in Appendix C. We use the coefficient estimates to derive estimates of the mean effect of FERS on separation rates. We predict that FERS would reduce the separation rate by 2 percentage points, a difference that is both large and statistically different from zero at the 1 percent level.[1] Since the predicted separation rate for those covered by CSRS is 4.4 percent, the predicted separation rate for those covered by FERS is 2.4 percent. Consequently, our results indicate that average separation rates for junior and mid-career personnel under FERS are 45 percent or nearly half the rates of those covered by CSRS, all else equal.

The difference in predicted separation rates between FERS and CSRS is fairly constant across age groups. The differences for each age group, shown in Figure 5.1, is about 2 percentage points.[2] Because of some data problems in determining separations and YOS, we examined how our results would change when alternative definitions of these variables are used. We found that our main result was robust—i.e., we

---

[1]A likelihood ratio test is used to determine the joint significance of the FERS parameter estimates. It should be noted that when we estimate Eq. 4.2 as a linear probability model, we find little difference in separation for those covered by FERS compared with those covered by CSRS. However, the linear probability model has several shortcomings that call into question the validity of this result. First, the error terms are heteroscedastic in a way that depends on the estimated coefficients. Second, the predicted probabilities are not constrained to lie between zero and one. Finally, since few individuals separate (less than 5 percent), the linear approximation to the true underlying distribution is not very good. Therefore, the logit results are more believable.

[2]The figure also shows predicted separation rates for those age 55 and older. While it is possible that these individuals separated from the civil service without a retirement benefit, it is also possible that these observations are miscoded, i.e., that these individuals are really retirees rather than separatees. Also, these predictions are made at the mean value of the other variables, including the FERS fiscal year dummies shown in Table 5.1.

Table 5.1

Logit Results, FERS Variables

Variable	Coefficient Estimate	Std. Error	Estimated Effect
FERS	−0.0886	0.1235	−0.01950
FY90* FERS	0.1313*	0.1187	0.0011
FY91* FERS	−0.9076**	0.1018	−0.0176
FY92* FERS	−0.9550**	0.1121	−0.0183
FY93* FERS	−1.0207**	0.1102	−0.0191
FY94* FERS	−0.6505**	0.1257	−0.01444
FY95* FERS	−0.7468**	0.1262	−0.0157
FY96* FERS	0.4942*	0.2176	0.0122
Age 26 to 30* FERS	−0.1389*	0.0611	−0.0053
Age 31 to 35* FERS	−0.1557	0.0643	−0.0057
Age 36 to 40* FERS	−0.0225	0.0773	−0.0027
Age 41 to 45* FERS	−0.1147	0.0790	−0.0048
Age 46 to 50* FERS	−0.1156	0.0787	−0.0048
Age 51 to 55* FERS	−0.2160*	0.0855	−0.0069
Age 56 to 60* FERS	−0.1315	0.0968	−0.0051
Age 61 to 65* FERS	−0.0319	0.1324	−0.0029
Age 66 up* FERS	−0.2197	0.2485	−0.0069

** statistically significant at the 1 percent level.
* statistically significant at the 5 percent level.
NOTE: The full regression results are reported in Appendix C.

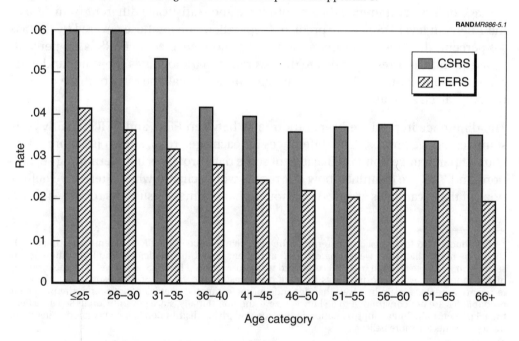

Figure 5.1—Estimated Separation Rates by Age Category Under Each System

continued to find that predicted separation rates were about 2 percentage points lower under FERS for those in their early and mid-careers.[3]

In Chapter Two, we found that FERS embeds weaker separation incentives for junior and mid-career civil service personnel. The empirical results above are not only consistent with these theoretical findings, but they indicate that the difference in separation rates is sizable. However, it should be recalled that our empirical approach uses a proxy control group that may not correctly control for differences in separation rates between fiscal years. If junior and mid-career personnel experienced bigger changes in separation rates than did senior personnel between the early 1980s and late 1980s and early 1990s because of environmental factors, then our approach will underestimate the difference in separate rates between FERS and CSRS. Similarly, if junior and mid-career personnel experienced smaller changes than did senior personnel, our approach will overestimate the differences in separation rates between FERS and CSRS.

Although our ability to deal with such biases is severely limited, it is useful to try to understand which direction the bias might take. Therefore, to get a feel for whether junior and mid-career personnel experienced bigger or smaller differences in separation rates than senior personnel, we show in Table 5.2 the mean separation rates for those who are covered by FERS and those covered by CSRS by year and by seniority. Separation rates varied over time for both the more-junior and more-senior personnel. For junior and mid-career personnel, separation rates rose from 5.6 percent in

Table 5.2

Mean Separation Rates by Year, Seniority, and Retirement System

Fiscal Year	Seniority	Retirement System	Mean Separation Rate
1983	Junior/mid-career	CSRS	0.056
1989	Junior/mid-career	FERS	0.078
1990	Junior/mid-career	FERS	0.079
1991	Junior/mid-career	FERS	0.074
1992	Junior/mid-career	FERS	0.052
1993	Junior/mid-career	FERS	0.053
1994	Junior/mid-career	FERS	0.052
1995	Junior/mid-career	FERS	0.057
1996	Junior/mid-career	FERS	0.042
1983	Senior	CSRS	0.0062
1989	Senior	CSRS	0.0094
1990	Senior	CSRS	0.0070
1991	Senior	CSRS	0.0193
1992	Senior	CSRS	0.0141
1993	Senior	CSRS	0.0172
1994	Senior	CSRS	0.0128
1995	Senior	CSRS	0.0164
1996	Senior	CSRS	0.0042

---

[3]According to DMDC, the educational variables are not always updated in the civilian personnel files as individuals accumulate more education. We examined how our results would change if the education variables were omitted and found no difference.

FY83 to 7.9 percent in FY90 and then declined over time to 4.2 percent in FY96. For senior personnel, separation rates rose from 0.6 percent in FY83 to 1.9 percent in FY91, remained at a higher level until FY95, and then fell to 0.4 percent in FY96.

As indicated by Table 5.2, the changes in separation rates for senior personnel between FY83 and FY96 tend to be larger in percentage terms than the changes in separation rates for junior and mid-career personnel over this period. Therefore, the estimated differences in separation rates produced by our model are likely overstated. Put differently, the 45 percent difference between those covered by FERS and those covered by CSRS estimated by our model likely overstates the true difference in separation rates between those covered by the two systems. Another reason to believe that our model likely overstates the difference is that past empirical research shows that civil service personnel are not highly responsive to differences in ACOL values. A study by Black, Moffitt, and Warner (1990a and 1990b) finds that separation is inelastic with respect to the ACOL variable in their analysis of separation behavior of DoD civil service personnel. This result suggests that the differences in separation rates between those covered by FERS and CSRS should not be large.

We therefore conclude from our empirical analysis that those junior and mid-career civil service personnel covered by FERS have lower separation rates than they would have had if they had been covered by CSRS. At most, the difference in separation rates is 2 percentage points, which represents a 45 percent difference in our data.

Chapter Six

SUMMARY AND CONCLUSIONS

It has sometimes been suggested that FERS induces more turnover among those in their mid- and late careers while at the same time inducing individuals, especially those in managerial positions, to retire at later ages. The purpose of our analysis was to examine whether the separation and retirement incentives embedded in FERS are consistent with these hypotheses. In the process of addressing these issues we also examined how FERS compares with CSRS in terms of providing greater expected lifetime wealth, whether FERS and CSRS embed different retirement incentives in general, and whether CSRS personnel have an incentive to switch to FERS.

When FERS was introduced, some civil service workers expressed concern that FERS would provide smaller benefits than CSRS for employees who planned to remain in the civil service until retirement (GAO, 1998). Our results suggest that this is generally not the case. We find FERS to be more generous than CSRS because expected lifetime wealth is predicted to be greater. The greater benefits under FERS might compensate civil service personnel for the risk they bear that their fund accumulations, or the returns on them, might fall because of a downturn in interest rates or in the stock market.

Our analysis of retirement incentives indicates that FERS will be more successful than CSRS at inducing individuals to retire at later ages in future years. We find that the age-YOS retirement incentives that are embedded in FERS and CSRS are the same, given our assumption that those covered by FERS face a minimum retirement age of 55. The MRA is 55 for those born before 1948 and rises gradually to 57 for those born after 1970. When the MRA is 57, we find that the age-YOS retirement incentives embedded in FERS and CSRS are not the same. In this case, we find that individuals who spend their careers in the civil service will retire later (at age 57 compared with age 55) if they are covered by FERS than if they are covered by CSRS. Since recent hires are more likely to be born after 1970, our analysis predicts that recent hires will retire at a later age under FERS than they would have retired had they been covered under CSRS. Therefore, we expect that the average retirement age will rise in the future as new hires age and eventually retire from the civil service.

Our analysis also suggests that FERS will create more variance in retirement ages, although the average retirement age is predicted to be the same, given an MRA of 55. We find that the penalty for deviating from the optimal retirement age is smaller under FERS. Those who retire earlier or who retire later than the optimal age will not lose as much in net earnings and retirement wealth by failing to retire at the wealth-maximizing retirement age under FERS. While FERS is more likely than CSRS to encourage senior personnel to stay in the civil service rather than retire at age 55, it is also more likely to encourage them to leave earlier. This aspect of FERS is not consistent with earlier hypotheses regarding the retirement incentives embedded in FERS. If the goal is to retain more senior personnel, then the retirement system needs to be constructed such that the optimal retirement age shifts up for them.

We also find that the generosity of FERS gives junior and mid-career employees an incentive to stay that is stronger than it would have been had they been under CSRS. Separation incentives are weaker under FERS for those in their early and mid-careers because the cost of leaving is greater under FERS. In contrast, for those nearing retirement, we find that separation incentives are stronger under FERS than they are under CSRS. Whether the stronger separation incentives for these personnel are sufficient to offset the weaker separation incentive for those in their mid-careers is an open question. Since greater turnover in the more-senior ranks provides greater promotion opportunities for those in the junior ranks, whether FERS provides greater or fewer promotion opportunities overall is also unclear.

Empirically, we estimate that the separation rate of early- and mid-career civil service personnel under FERS is 45 percent lower than the rate for similar early- and mid-career personnel under CSRS. It is likely that this estimate overstates the difference in separation rates. The bias arises because of difficulties in disentangling empirically the effect of FERS on separation rates from the effect of changes in environment factors in general on separation rates. Nonetheless, our empirical analysis suggests that separation rates are not higher for early and mid-career under FERS, contrary to the initial intent of FERS, and appear to be substantially lower.

These results suggest that turnover targets for junior and mid-career personnel need to be pursued outside of the retirement benefits package since the current retirement systems are not producing the desired turnover results. Determining how effective other forms of compensation, such as separation pay, would be in meeting these targets should be an area for future research.

As for switching to FERS, we find that those who face the switch decision early in their careers are better off financially by switching, given our assumption of a 6 percent real return on the TSP. Those who face this decision later in their careers are not better off if they plan to stay in the civil service until they retire.

These results have implications for the switch window opened during the second half of 1998 for employees covered by CSRS.[1] Since those covered by CSRS in 1998 would not be in their early or mid-careers but would have at least 14 YOS, our results suggest these individuals would generally be worse off by switching to FERS if they plan to stay in the civil service until retirement.

---

[1]There were no data yet available for 1998 as of the writing of this report.

However, at higher assumed rates, such as a 15 percent real return on the TSP fund, we predict that they *would* be better off financially by having switched. Therefore, whether many more individuals than expected switched to FERS in 1998 depended crucially on what these individuals believed about the future real return on the TSP. Given the enormous growth in the stock market returns in recent years, individuals facing the switch decision may have believed that such returns could be earned over the rest of their careers. In that case, larger numbers than might otherwise have been expected may have choosen to switch to FERS. Since FERS costs more to the agencies that employ them (GAO, 1998), differences in the number of individuals who switched could have important cost implications for these agencies.

SUMMARY OF FERS AND CSRS

This appendix summarizes the main features of FERS and CSRS (Office of Personnel Management, 1998).

FERS

FERS became effective on January 1, 1987. Most employees who are hired after December 31, 1983, are covered by FERS. Others have the option to switch to FERS if they meet certain requirements. FERS consists of three components: the Basic Plan, the Thrift Savings Plan, and Social Security.

Basic Plan

The Basic Benefit Plan (or the Basic Plan) vests members at five YOS. Under this plan, individuals contribute the difference between 7 percent of their basic pay and the Social Security OASDI (Old-Age, Survivors, and Disability Insurance) tax rate. In 1998, this percentage was 0.8 percent. Individuals may get a refund of these contributions with interest instead of the retirement annuity when they leave federal service. The contribution rate will rise gradually beginning in 1999 until it reaches 1.3 percent in 2001. However, the increases will be in effect only through December 2002.

The benefit formula under the Basic Plan equals 1 percent of an individual's highest three-year average pay times their YOS. If the individual retires at or beyond age 62 with 20 or more YOS, the formula is 1.1 percent of their highest three-year average pay times YOS.

The normal age of retirement (i.e., the age when an individual can leave service and begin collecting the annuity) depends on the member's YOS. The schedule is shown in Table A.1. For those with five YOS, the normal retirement age is 62. For those with 20 YOS, the normal age is 60. For those with 30 YOS, the normal age is the minimum retirement age. The MRA is between 55 and 57, depending on the employee's date of birth, as shown in Table A.2. Those who have 10 YOS can also retire at their MRA, but their benefit is reduced at the rate of 5 percent for each year that the individual is under age 62 if he or she is not eligible for an immediate annuity.

Table A.1

**Normal Age of Retirement
Under FERS Basic Plan**

Age	YOS
62	5
60	20
MRA (age 55–57)[a]	10
MRA (age 55–57)[b]	30

[a]Reduced benefit.

[b]The allowed normal retirement age depends on date of birth.

Table A.2

Minimum Retirement Age

If date of birth is	MRA is
Before 1948	55
In 1948	55 and 2 months
In 1949	55 and 4 months
In 1950	55 and 6 months
In 1951	55 and 8 months
In 1952	55 and 10 months
In 1953 through 1964	56
In 1965	56 and 2 months
In 1966	56 and 4 months
In 1967	56 and 6 months
In 1968	56 and 8 months
In 1969	56 and 10 months
In 1970 or after	57

The Basic Plan also allows for early retirement and for deferred retirement. An early retirement benefit is available for those who are voluntarily separated as part of reduction-in-force (RIF) or, under some circumstances, who are involuntarily separated. To be eligible, the individual must be either age 50 with 20 YOS or any age with 25 YOS. Those who leave before reaching a normal retirement age are eligible to receive a deferred retirement benefit. The deferred retirement age and YOS are the same as those shown in Table A.1. For example, an individual who leaves civil service at age 45 with 20 YOS would not be eligible for either normal or early retirement benefits but would be eligible for deferred retirement. This individual could begin collecting benefits at age 60.[1]

Individuals who meet certain requirements also get a special retirement supplement, which is paid until the individual reaches age 62. This supplement approximately equals the Social Security benefit that the individual earns from being employed in the federal government. To be eligible for the supplement immediately, the individual must retire on or after the MRA with 30 YOS or at age 60 with 20 YOS. Alternatively, the individual can receive the supplement if he or she retires early as part of a

---

[1]Those with 10 YOS can claim a deferred retirement benefit at their MRA, but their annuity is reduced at the rate of 5 percent for each year that they are under age 62.

RIF and meets the age and service requirements (age 50 with 20 YOS or any age with 25 YOS).

The Basic Plan also gives a cost-of-living adjustment to those age 62 and older and to those who retire on a disability annuity. This adjustment equals the change in the Consumer Price Index (CPI) if the change in the CPI is less than or equal to 2 percent. It equals 2 percent if the change in the CPI is between 2 and 3 percent and equals the percentage change in the CPI minus 1 percent if the change in the CPI exceeds 3 percent.

Thrift Savings Plan

The Thrift Savings Plan is a defined contribution plan that shares many features with the 401(k) pension plans found in the private sector. Under the plan, the government makes automatic and matching contributions to a fund and the employee has several options for investing the fund, including investing it in a government securities fund, a common stock fund, or a fixed income index fund (or some combination of the three). The government's automatic contribution for each member is 1 percent of the member's basic pay for which the employee is vested after three years. The government matches 100 percent of the employee's contribution for the first 3 percent; 50 percent of the employee's contributions for the next 2 percent; 0 percent of the employee's contributions above 5 percent. An individual can contribute a maximum of 10 percent of basic pay each pay period subject to Internal Revenue Service restrictions. Individuals are immediately vested in their own contributions, and their contributions (and earnings from all the contributions) are tax deferred.

The Thrift Savings Plan has several provisions for withdrawing funds. With the exception of age-based in-service withdrawal and financial hardship in-service withdrawal, members can withdraw the balance of their account only if they leave federal service. The withdrawal options depend on whether the member is eligible for retirement benefits under the Basic Plan, as determined by his or her age and completed YOS. If the member is ineligible for an immediate annuity and separates from federal service, he or she must transfer the vested account balance of the TSP to an Individual Retirement Account (IRA) or other eligible retirement plan.[2] There are two cases in which the member can withdraw TSP funds while in service. If the individual is 59.5 or older, he or she can withdraw all or part of the account balance. This is called age-based in-service withdrawal. In the other case, if the individual demonstrates financial hardship, he or she can withdraw his or her own contributions and the earnings on those contributions.

Members have three withdrawal options. First, the employee can transfer the account balance to an IRA. Second, he or she can receive a cash lump sum or a series of equal payments. Finally, those who separate can purchase a life annuity, which can begin at the date of separation or at a later date. If the member chooses the first

---

[2]This is true if the account balance exceeds $3,500. If the balance is $3,500 or less, the member receives an immediate lump sum cash payment.

option, he or she faces a 10 percent penalty for withdrawing from the IRA before age 59.5. If the member chooses option 2, there is a penalty if the member receives any proceeds before age 55 equal to 10 percent of the amount received before age 59.5.

Social Security Benefits

Individuals covered by FERS also have OASDI coverage and Medicare coverage. (Greater details are provided by the Social Security Administration, 1998). Individuals covered by OASDI are eligible for monthly benefits if they retire and are at least age 62. To be eligible, the employee must pay Social Security taxes for 40 quarters.

The amount of the employee's benefits depends in part on average earnings upon which Social Security taxes have been paid. These average earnings are adjusted for changes in average earnings that have occurred for the American workforce in general. The benefits also depend on the employee's family composition (e.g., whether or not the individual has a spouse that is eligible for benefits) and on CPI changes that occur after the individual becomes entitled to claim benefits. Since taxable earnings on which the benefits are based are subject to a maximum, the benefits are de facto limited as well.

Each year, individuals are required to contribute 6.2 percent of their earnings for OASDI up to a maximum wage base. The contribution is made by way of a payroll tax. The maximum wage base was $68,400 for 1998. It increases each year since average earnings of U.S. workers increase each year. The Medicare portion of Social Security requires an additional contribution rate of 1.45 percent of earnings. These taxes are matched by the employing agency. The Medicare portion is not capped.

CSRS

CSRS consists only of a defined benefit plan. CSRS benefits are vested after five YOS. In 1998, individuals contributed 7 percent of their earnings to CSRS. As a result of the Balanced Budget Act of 1997, the CSRS contribution rate will rise to 7.5 percent by 2001 and will stay at that level through December 2002. An individual who leaves with more than one YOS and fewer than five YOS may get a refund of these contributions with interest instead of the retirement annuity when he or she leaves federal service, if he or she is not eligible for an immediate annuity.

The benefit formula under CSRS equals 1.5 percent of an individual's highest three-year average earnings times his or her YOS for the first five YOS, plus 1.75 percent of the highest-three average earnings times YOS for the next five YOS, plus 2 percent of the highest-three average earnings times all YOS and months over 10. The maximum annuity an individual can receive is 80 percent of the highest-three average earnings. Normally, this is acquired after 41 years and 11 months of credible civilian and military service. Unused sick leave may increase the 80 percent maximum. The CSRS benefit formula provides a greater benefit than does the Basic Plan formula under FERS, holding YOS constant.

The normal ages and YOS for retirement are shown in Table A.3. CSRS does not have an MRA like FERS does. Unlike FERS, individuals under CSRS with 10 YOS can retire only at age 62. Individuals subject to voluntary separation during a RIF or, in some circumstances, involuntary separation are eligible for an early retirement benefit. Early retirement is available to those who are age 50 with 20 YOS or who are any age with 25 YOS. CSRS also offers deferred retirement but only at age 62 for those with at least five YOS. Therefore, an individual who leaves at age 45 with 10 YOS could retire under CSRS at age 62. This deferred retirement age is older than the ages for those covered by FERS.

CSRS annuities are fully inflation protected. The annuitant receives a COLA adjustment each year equal to the change in the CPI.

Table A.3

Normal Age of Retirement Under CSRS

Age	YOS
62	5
60	20
55	30

PROBLEMS WITH THE NONSEQUENTIAL YOS VARIABLE IN DOD CIVIL SERVICE DATA

We detected some inconsistencies in the reporting of the YOS variable in the civilian personnel files. To examine the reliability of the YOS variable, we first strung together the yearly inventories from FY81 to FY96, by individual record ID number, and examined how the YOS variable changed from fiscal year to fiscal year. What we hoped to find was that the variable would generally increment by one as fiscal year increased by one. In most cases, this is what occurred. However, for a nontrivial number of cases, this did not occur; for these, YOS increased and decreased in ways that made no sense. Table B.1 gives some examples of different cases that we observed. Each cell indicates the YOS for the individual in the particular fiscal year. For example, for case 91, YOS is 27 in the FY81 file, 26 in the FY82 file, 16 in the FY83 file, and so forth. These cases are just a small fraction of the total cases and serve to illustrate the issue.

Of the 797,785 individuals in the 1995 inventory (net of the exclusions defined in Chapter Five), we found that 18.5 percent of, or 147,802, cases had nonsequential YOS in one or more of the previous inventories.

Table B.2 presents some of the key characteristics of the nonsequential cases in FY95. We find that 69 percent of the cases are veterans. This figure exceeds the overall representation of veterans in the FY95 inventory; in the (net) inventory as a whole, 41

Table B.1

Examples of Nonsequential YOS Cases

Case Number								Fiscal Year								
	81	82	83	84	85	86	87	88	89	90	91	92	93	94	95	96
91	27	26	16	17	18	19	20	21								
104	3	4	5			0	1	2	3	4	11	12	13	14	15	16
125	15	16	15	16	18	19										
135	9	10	11	12	13	14	15	16	17	18	19	20	21	15	16	17
143	3	4	15	16	17	9	10	11	12	13	14	15	16	17		
150	5	6	7	13	14	15	16	17								
169	7	8	12	13	14	15	16	17	18	19	20	21	22	16	17	
182	0	0	0	0	0	0	0	18	19	20	21	22	23	24	25	26

NOTES: Cells indicate the YOS for the particular case for each year. Cells that are blank indicate no information available for that year.

percent are veterans. We also find that 43 percent are in the Air Force, whereas only 22 percent of the FY95 inventory as a whole are Air Force personnel. Therefore, Air Force personnel are overrepresented among the nonsequential cases. The nonsequential cases are also concentrated among a small subset of defense agencies. In fact, 66 percent of the nonsequential cases are accounted for by 18 agencies/bureaus (see Table B.2). A large number of cases are in the Air Materiel Command. Finally, of the 98,499 cases that are accounted for by these 18 agencies, about 75 percent are veterans.

The figures in Table B.2 suggest that specific agencies, particularly in the Air Force, have difficulty consistently reporting the YOS of veterans.

Table B.2

Key Characteristics of Nonsequential YOS Cases in FY95
(numbers and percentages)

Characteristic	Total		Veterans	
	Number	Percentage of Cases	Number	Percentage of Total
Total	147,802	100.00%	102,256	69.18%
Air Force	64,075	43.35%	55,229	86.19%
Bureau				
Headquarters, Air Force Reserve	9,933	6.72%	9,414	94.80%
Aerospace Defense Command	4,622	3.13%	3,855	83.41%
Air Training Command	4,594	3.11%	3,827	83.30%
Air Force Southern Command	3,450	2.33%	2,886	83.65%
Air National Guard Units	5,380	3.64%	3,248	60.37%
Air Materiel Command	26,728	18.08%	24,303	90.93%
U.S. Army Corps of Engineers	3,356	2.27%	1,645	49.02%
U.S. Army Forces Command	5,730	3.88%	4,102	71.59%
U.S. Army Medical Command	5,124	3.47%	2,411	47.05%
Army National Guard Units	5,754	4.89%	3,317	54.52%
U.S. Army Training and Doctrine Command	4,128	2.79%	2,776	67.25%
U.S. Navy Sea Systems Command	5,172	3.50%	3,281	63.44%
Naval Air Systems Command	3,530	2.39%	2,405	68.13%
Naval Facilities Engineering Command	2,715	1.84%	1,697	62.51%
Defense Logistics Agency	4,874	3.30%	3,058	62.74%
Dependents School	3,409	2.31%	1,143	33.53%
Defense Commissary Agency	4,522	3.06%	1,828	40.43%
Defense Finance and Accounting Service	2,534	1.71%	1,118	44.12%
Total bureau	98,499	66.43%	73,190	74.31%

VARIABLE DEFINITIONS, DESCRIPTIVE STATISTICS, AND
REGRESSION RESULTS

Table C.1 presents the definition of the variables used in the empirical analysis, their means, and the full logit regression results presented in Chapter Five.

Table C.1

Variable Definitions, Sample Proportions, Logit Results

Variable	Equals 1 if	Proportion	Coefficient Estimate	Std. Error
FERS	Covered by FERS	0.617	−0.0886	0.1235
BLUECOLL	PATCO = blue collar	0.224	−0.3414**	0.0695
PROFESSL	PATCO = professional	0.201	−0.7240**	0.0490
ADMINIST	PATCO = administrative	0.208	−0.7358**	0.0469
TECHNICL	PATCO = technical	0.145	−0.5956**	0.0405
CLERICAL	PATCO = clerical	0.205	−0.5531**	0.0378
AIRFORCE	Agency = Air Force	0.234	−0.1848**	0.0283
ARMY	Agency = Army	0.327	0.2472**	0.0253
NAVY	Agency = Navy	0.307	0.0927**	0.0255
MARINES	Agency = Marine Corps	0.018	−0.0010	0.0572
SUP_MGR	Position is supervisory, managerial, or individual is a supervisory official (CSRA), management official (CSRA), or leader	0.133	0.1285**	0.0340
GSPLAN	Pay Plan = general schedule	0.714	0.3291**	0.0570
WGPLAN	Pay Plan = wage grade	0.178	0.0278**	0.0489
RATING2	Rating of Record = exceeds fully successful	0.319	0.0744**	0.0206
RATING3	Rating of Record = fully successful	0.241	0.3108**	0.0217
RATING4	Rating of Record = minimally successful	0.002	1.1538**	0.1031
RATING5	Rating of Record = unsatisfactory	0.001	1.0046**	0.1430
RATING6	Rating of Record = cannot be rated	0.161	0.4274**	0.0253
GRADE1	Grade = 1	0.002	0.3276**	0.1252
GRADE2	Grade = 2	0.008	0.2112*	0.0966
GRADE3	Grade = 3	0.034	−0.0464	0.0889
GRADE4	Grade = 4	0.094	−0.1436	0.0866
GRADE5	Grade = 5	0.140	−0.2461**	0.0850
GRADE6	Grade = 6	0.062	−0.4030**	0.0878
GRADE7	Grade = 7	0.084	−0.4453**	0.0850
GRADE8	Grade = 8	0.045	−0.2891**	0.0889
GRADE9	Grade = 9	0.104	−0.3958**	0.0842
GRADE10	Grade = 10	0.062	−0.3566**	0.0884
GRADE11	Grade = 11	0.133	−0.5130**	0.0844
GRADE12	Grade = 12	0.134	−0.5963**	0.0850
GRADE13	Grade = 13	0.055	−0.4281**	0.0867
GRADE14	Grade = 14	0.026	−0.4151**	0.1035

Table C.1—continued

Variable	Equals 1 if	Proportion	Coefficient Estimate	Std. Error
INFLOW1	Entered inventory during last FY (hire or rehire)	0.079	0.4783**	0.0230
BELOWHS	Education level = less than high school degree	0.035	−0.0298	0.0506
HS_GED	Education level = high school graduate or GED	0.327	−0.1127**	0.0261
AADEG	Education level = AA degree	0.048	−0.0831*	0.0379
SOMECOLL	Education level = college but no degree	0.283	−0.0904**	0.0258
MA_PLUS	Education level = Master's, post-master's, professional, or post-professional degree	0.058	0.1706**	0.0344
PHD	Education level = PhD or post-PhD	0.009	0.1915*	0.0803
BLACK	Race = non-Hispanic black	0.148	−0.0603**	0.0196
HISPANIC	Race = Hispanic	0.056	−0.1899**	0.0332
INDIAN	Race (minority group) = American Indian or Alaskan Native	0.008	0.1777**	0.0695
PACIFIC	Race (minority group) = Asian or Pacific Islander	0.049	−0.3581**	0.0354
FEMALE	Gender = female	0.377	0.2452**	0.0195
HANDICAP	Reported medical disability	0.084	−0.0957**	0.0283
DMDCVET	Military veteran as defined by DMDC	0.402	0.1190**	0.0207
NEWENG	OPM region = RI, VT, CT, ME, MA, NH	0.033	0.2805**	0.0364
EASTERN	OPM region = NJ, NY, PR, VA	0.052	−0.0110	0.0332
S_EAST	OPM region = AL, FL, GA, KY, MS, NC, SC, TN	0.167	−0.2165**	0.0241
G_LAKES	OPM region = WI, OH, MN, MI, ID, IL	0.100	−0.1940**	0.0284
S_WEST	OPM region = TX, AK, LA, OK, NM	0.120	−0.0483	0.0285
MID_CONT	OPM region = IA, KS, MO, NE	0.032	−0.1382**	0.0431
ROCKIES	OPM region = CA, Samoa, AZ, Guam, HI, NV	0.042	0.2018**	0.0378
WESTERN	OPM region = WY, SD, UT, ND, MT, CO	0.171	0.2545**	0.0222
N_WEST	OPM region = AK, ID, OR, WA	0.036	0.1161**	0.0379
YOS2	YOS = 2	0.046	0.4251**	0.0286
YOS3	YOS = 3	0.052	0.3324**	0.0290
YOS4	YOS = 4	0.063	0.2894**	0.0279
YOS5	YOS = 5	0.070	0.2471**	0.0275
YOS6	YOS = 6	0.066	0.1942**	0.0294
YOS7	YOS = 7	0.059	0.0938**	0.0325
YOS8	YOS = 8	0.049	0.1103**	0.0353
YOS9	YOS = 9	0.043	−0.0318	0.0395
YOS10	YOS = 10	0.033	−0.0462	0.0448
YOS11	YOS = 11	0.024	−0.1223*	0.0533
YOS12	YOS = 12	0.014	−0.3032**	0.0767
YOS24	YOS = 24	0.010	−1.4739**	0.1793
YOS25	YOS = 25	0.015	−1.2760**	0.1480
YOS26	YOS = 26	0.019	−1.6645**	0.1408
YOS27	YOS = 27	0.022	−1.8019**	0.1388
YOS28	YOS = 28	0.025	−1.8166**	0.1342
YOS29	YOS = 29	0.026	−1.7780**	0.1328
YOS30	YOS = 30	0.026	−1.7181**	0.1306
YOS31UP	YOS = 31 and higher	0.133	−1.5925**	0.1102
YR89	Fiscal year = 1989	0.101	0.3615**	0.1140
YR90	Fiscal year = 1990	0.111	0.2964*	0.1232
YR91	Fiscal year = 1991	0.112	1.4246**	0.1064
YR92	Fiscal year = 1992	0.111	1.1291**	0.1155
YR93	Fiscal year = 1993	0.111	1.3171**	0.1132
YR94	Fiscal year = 1994	0.103	1.0535**	0.1284
YR95	Fiscal year = 1995	0.100	1.3365**	0.1289
YR96	Fiscal year = 1996	0.095	−0.0923	0.2187
FYR90	Fiscal year = 1990 and covered by FERS	0.070	0.4942	0.2176
FYR91	Fiscal year = 1991 and covered by FERS	0.076	−0.7468**	0.1262
FYR92	Fiscal year = 1992 and covered by FERS	0.081	−0.6505**	0.1257
FYR93	Fiscal year = 1993 and covered by FERS	0.084	−1.0207**	0.1102

Table C.1—continued

Variable	Equals 1 if	Proportion	Coefficient Estimate	Std. Error
FYR94	Fiscal year = 1994 and covered by FERS	0.084	−0.9550**	0.1121
FYR95	Fiscal year = 1995 and covered by FERS	0.085	−0.9076**	0.1018
FYR96	Fiscal year = 1996 and covered by FERS	0.084	0.1313*	0.1187
AGE26_30	age is less than 31	0.144	−0.0044	0.0562
AGE31_35	age is between 31 and 35	0.134	−0.1259*	0.0594
AGE36_40	age is between 36 and 40	0.101	−0.3824**	0.0724
AGE41_45	age is between 41 and 45	0.110	−0.4373**	0.0738
AGE46_50	age is between 46 and 50	0.146	−0.5390**	0.0720
AGE51_55	age is between 51 and 55	0.150	−0.5048**	0.0757
AGE56_60	age is between 56 and 60	0.089	−0.4894**	0.0823
AGE61_65	age is between 61 and 65	0.037	−0.5983**	0.1026
AGE66_UP	age is 66 or over	0.013	−0.5514**	0.1344
FAGE2630	age is less than 31 and covered by FERS	0.121	−0.1389*	0.0611
FAGE3135	age is between 31 and 35 and covered by FERS	0.111	−0.1557*	0.0643
FAGE3640	age is between 36 and 40 and covered by FERS	0.087	−0.0225	0.0773
FAGE4145	age is between 41 and 45 and covered by FERS	0.085	−0.1147	0.0790
FAGE4650	age is between 46 and 50 and covered by FERS	0.072	−0.1156	0.0787
FAGE5155	age is between 51 and 55 and covered by FERS	0.046	−0.2160	0.0855
FAGE5660	age is between 56 and 60 and covered by FERS	0.024	−0.1315	0.0968
FAGE6165	age is between 61 and 65 and covered by FERS	0.008	−0.0319	0.1324
FAGE66UP	age is 66 or over and covered by FERS	0.001	−0.2197	0.2485
INTERCEPT		1	−2.9070**	0.1114
−2 LOG LIKELIHOOD			185,176**	
SEPARATE	separated during fiscal year	0.041		

** statistically significant at the 1 percent level.

* statistically significant at the 5 percent level.

NOTES: The number of observations is 537,164. The omitted categories are CSRS, other white collar, other defense agency, other pay plans, nonsupervisors or managers, rating of record is 1, grade 15, non-inflow, college graduate, white, male, nondisability worker, nonveteran, mid-Atlantic region, YOS 1, FY83, FY89, covered by CSRS, age group less than 26, age group less than 26 and covered by FERS. OPM = office of personnel management.

Asch, Beth J., and John T. Warner, *A Theory of Military Compensation and Personnel Policy*, Santa Monica, Calif.: RAND, MR-439-OSD, 1994.

Black, Matthew, Robert Moffitt, and John Warner, "The Dynamics of Job Separation: The Case of Federal Employees," *Journal of Applied Econometrics*, Vol. 5, pp. 245–262, 1990a.

———, "Reply to Comment by Glenn Gotz on 'The Dynamics of Job Separation: The Case of Federal Employees,'" *Journal of Applied Econometrics*, Vol. 5, pp. 269–272, 1990b.

Causer, Mike, "Oops, Wrong Pension Plan," *Washington Post*, p. B-2, February 27, 1998.

Congressional Budget Office, *Employee Turnover in the Federal Government*, Washington, D.C., February 1986.

Daula, Thomas, and Robert Moffitt, "Estimating Dynamic Models of Quit Behavior: The Case of Military Reenlistment," *Journal of Labor Economics*, Vol. 13, No. 3, 1995.

Federal Retirement Thrift Investment Board, "Analysis of 1996 Thrift Savings Plan Participant Demographics," Washington, D.C., 1996.

General Accounting Office (GAO), *The Federal Employees' Retirement System: Potential Changes in Agency Retirement Costs Following an Open Season, Testimony November 5, 1997*, Washington, D.C., GAO/T-GGD-98-27, 1998.

———, *Federal Retirement: Federal and Private Sector Retirement Program Benefits Vary*, Washington, D.C., GAO/GGD-97-40, April 1997.

———, *Federal Retirement: Implementation of the Federal Employees Retirement System*, Washington, D.C., GAO/GGD-88-107, August 4, 1988.

———, *Recruitment and Retention: Inadequate Federal Pay Cited as Primary Problem by Agency Officials*, Washington, D.C., GAO/GGD-90-117, September 1990.

Gotz, Glenn, "Comment on 'The Dynamics of Job Separation: The Case of Federal Employees,'" *Journal of Applied Econometrics*, Vol. 5, pp. 263–268, 1990.

Gotz, Glenn, and John McCall, *A Dynamic Retention Model for Air Force Officers: Theory and Estimates*, Santa Monica, Calif.: RAND, R-3028-AF, 1980.

Johnston, William B., *Civil Service 2000*, Washington, D.C.: U.S. Office of Personnel Management Career Entry Group, June 1988.

Lazear, Edward, and Robert Moore, "Pensions and Turnover," in *Pensions in the U.S. Economy*, Zvi Bodie, ed., Chicago: University of Chicago Press, pp. 57–85, 1983.

Leonard, Herman, "The Federal Civil Service Retirement System: An Analysis of Its Financial Condition and Current Reform Proposals," in *Pensions, Labor, and Individual Choice*, David A. Wise, ed., Chicago: University of Chicago Press, pp. 399–443, 1985.

Lumsdaine, Robin, James Stock, and David A. Wise, "Three Models of Retirement: Computational Complexity Versus Predictive Validity," in *Topics in the Economics of Aging*, David A. Wise, ed., Chicago: University of Chicago Press, pp. 19–57, 1992.

Mace, Don, and Eric Yoder, *Federal Employees Almanac 1995*, Washington, D.C.: Federal Employees News Digest, 1995.

Office of Personnel Management, *CSRS and FERS Handbooks for Personnel and Payroll Offices*, Government Printing Office, Washington, D.C., or http://www.opm.gov/asd/htm/hod.htm, 1998.

Office of the Secretary of Defense (OSD), "Basic Design of the Federal Employees Retirement System (FERS)," memo provided by the Office of the Deputy Assistant Secretary of Defense for Civilian Personnel Policy, 1997.

Rust, John, "A Dynamic Programming Model of Retirement Behavior," in *The Economics of Aging*, David A. Wise, ed., Chicago: University of Chicago Press, pp. 205–224, 1989.

Social Security Administration, *Social Security Handbook*, Washington, D.C., 1998.

Stock, James H., and David A. Wise, "Pensions, the Option Value of Work, and Retirement," *Econometrica*, Vol. 58, No. 5, pp. 1151–1180, 1990.

Thrift Savings Plan Board, *Analysis of 1996 Thrift Savings Plan Participant Demographics*, Washington, D.C.: Federal Retirement Thrift Investment Board, 1997.

Warner, John, and Matthew Goldberg, "The Influence of Non-Pecuniary Factors on Labor Supply: The Case of Navy Enlisted Personnel," *Review of Economics and Statistics*, Vol. 66, No. 1, pp. 26–35, 1984.